Kathak Sagar

Kathak Sagar

Dr. Bharti Gupta

RADHA PUBLICATIONS
New Delhi - 110 002

First Edition 2004
Edition : 2019
ISBN : 81-7487-343-0

RADHA PUBLICATIONS
4378/4B, Ansari Road, Daryaganj
New Delhi-110 002
Phone : 23261839, 23254306

Published by Nitin Garg for Radha Publications and printed by Tarun Offset Printers, Mauzpur, Shahadra, Delhi.

PROLOGUE

I dedicate this book as an offering in the feet of mother Saraswati, Shri Ganesh, the Lord, Suryadev, Gurudev and my parents.

It is a matter of great pleasure that today educated class of the society has also started taking interest in the study, practice and experimenting with dance and music. Generally, the interest in classical dance has been growing.

Many books have been written on Kathak dance which are connected with the curriculum of various universities and these deserve praise.

My object in writing this book is that students at all levels may benefit and through self study clear the written examinations on Kathak. Since today education at all levels in the schools and universities has become complex, students do not have time to understand the theoretical aspects and teachers also do not give much importance to it.

In view of the above, I was inspired to write this book in which I have taken up various aspects of Kathak in minute details albeit in simple form and which I expect to be useful for students of first year to post graduate classes of various universities.

I have borrowed heavily in writing this book from various scriptures and books and I am grateful to all these scholars. I received much co-operation from my brother Shri Rakesh Gupta in writing this book and from my husband, Shri M. M. Agrawal in its English translation. I am thankful to them.

Much labour has gone into writing this book. If students do benefit I would consider the effort worth it.

I do expect that readers will adopt this book and encourage me to write further to serve the students and those involved with Kathak. I also submit to the learned readers and if there have been any mistakes or shortcomings in the book which might have crept inadvertently, they would forgive me but inform me to enable me to correct the same in future editions.

—Dr. Bharti Gupta

Contents

1

1. ORIGIN OF DANCE

When Satyug commenced after the end of Tretayug, the lorc of heavens, Indra once went to Brahmaji and requested him to advise some such means of entertainment for gods, which should be audible as well as visual *i.e.* which may be heard as well as seen.

Following the prayers by Indra and other gods, Brahmaji was pleased and formed a new Ved, taking the essence of the four Vedas. While subject selection (storyline) was made from Rigveda, music was contributed by Samveda, art of emoting (Abhinaya) from Yajurveda and 'Ragas' were taken from Athervaveda and thus a fifth Veda *i.e.* Natyaveda was born.

After delivering the Natyaveda, Brahmaji asked Indra that he should arrange for' Abhinaya' by gods and the art should be practiced by the gods who are skilled, elegant and adept in the art of speech. However, the gods expressed their inability in learning and practicing the art of 'Natya' and requested that this art be exhibited/ demonstrated by the sages *i.e.* Rishis.

Brahmaji then taught the Natyaveda to sage Bharat who taught the same to his hundred sons and made them enact the Natya before Brahmaji and also proposed the scheme of 'KaushikiVrutti'. Brahmaji then created Apsaras and gave them to sage Bharat for the purpose. In this way, 'Natya' was developed fully and the first performance of dance was made in the 'Indradhwaj' festival.

This performance depicted the defeat of Asurs (demons) and victory of gods but the Asurs were obviously displeased and created trouble during performance and by using their magical powers rendered the dancers standstill. Then, Indra removed the Asurs by using force and the need for a theatre (NatyaMandal) was felt. A new theatre was built by Vishwakarma and simultaneously Brahmaji made Asurs understand that 'dance' was not only a means of entertainment and pleasure but also a strong medium for depicting the Bhavas (feelings) of the entire universe and thereafter for the first time in a closed theatre, 'Amrut Manthan', a play was enacted.

The play received praise from gods and this made the sons of sage Bharat proud and they started ridiculing other sages. Aggrieved with this behavior, the sages cursed the sons of Bharat but when the gods requested them, they modified the curse to the extent that while the art of Natya would not perish, the residual curse would continue to remain effective.

After sometime, when King Nahusha attained the position of Indra, he requested sage Bharat to have the Natya performed by his sons on the earth as a result of which the curse on his sons would lose effect. Then the sons of the sage Bharat married the woman (Manushi Stri) and performed Natya on the earth as a result of which they were delivered of the curse and returned to the heavens.

2. TANDAVA AND LASYA

The Tandava dance form was originated by Lord Shiva. Lord Shiva has been credited with many dance forms; of these foremost is Tandava dance. According to 'Shivopasnadak', Shiva after killing the demon 'Tripurasur' went into rapture (ullas) and danced. This dance form was re-enacted by his disciple, 'Tandu' Muni who popularized it. This dance form, practised by Tandu Muni, came to be known as 'Tandava'. This dance form involves expressions reflecting Courage (Veerta), Extreme anger (Roudra), Hatred (Vibhatsa), Enjoyment (Anand) and Anger born out of grief and sympathy (Karuna Janit Krodh). To express these rasas, the dancer twists his limbs aggressively, which is not considered appropriate for the women. In the course of this dance, the fire of anger seems to peak, the earth seems to tremble as if the whole world is going through a process of destruction.

'Tandava' dance form has seven sub-classifications :

1. **'Tripur Tandava' :** The dance performed by Lord Shiva after killing the demon Tripurasur reflected Courage (Veerta) and Extreme anger (Roudra) and is known as 'Tripur Tandava'. The 'Bols' of this dance form are mostly in 'Adi Laya'.
2. **'Anand Tandava' :** After Shiva had slayed 'Tripurasur', Goddess Uma performed 'Lasya' dance which is an embodiment of Pleasure (Ullas) and Excitement (Umang) which pleased the angry Shiva. This dance is known as 'Anand Tandava'.
3. **'Gauri Tandava' :** In this dance form, Shiva and Parvati dance together in 'Shringar Rasa'.
4. **'Kalika Tandava' :** In order to destroy evil and wicked, Shiva dances expressing his Bhairav form, which is known as 'Kalika Tandava'.
5. **'Sandhya Tandava' :** After the death of his wife 'Sati', Shiva carried her dead body on his shoulders and danced while in

mourning. This dance starts with Karuna Rasa and ends with expressing Roudra (Extreme anger) and Bhayanak Rasa (Terrible). This dance form is known as 'SandhyaTandava'.

6. **'Uma Tandava'** : This dance form stresses the conjugal affection, love and attraction in its purest and simple form.
7. **'Samhar Tandava'** : The destruction of entire universe is reflected in 'Samhar Tandava'

The instruments played in Tandava are 'Nada Pradhan' (Percussion instruments) with echo effect, as if surrounding and enveloping entire environment; *e.g.* Ghariyal, Jhanjh, Dumroo, Mrudang, Chang, Dhausa, Naubat etc.

The appropriate costume for Tandava performance is usually 'Male' dress i.e. the dancer ties his hairs like a Jata (Bun) showing half moon and river Ganga and wears an 'Angvastram' akin to the lion skin worn by Lord Shiva. The dancer applies 'Tripunda' (a Shaiva sign) on his forehead, takes Trident in one hand and Dumroo in the other. He also applies Bhasmi (Ashes) on his body.

Lasya :

After the demon 'Tripurasur' was killed by Lord Shiva, he danced in rage *i.e.* Tandava. Then to pacify and please him, Goddess Uma performed a soft and Shringarik dance, which is called 'Lasya'. Goddess Uma taught this dance to Usha, the daughter of Daitya Banasur. She popularized this dance form in Vrindavan.

The dance is extremely soft in movements and shringarik in expressions and this is performed more effectively by female dancers. The Raas Nritya of Mathura, Halisak of South India, Kathak, Bharatnatyam, Manipuri, Oddissi, Mohiniattam, Kuchipudi etc, which are performed today in various regions owe their origin to 'Lasya'.

Three types of Lasya Nritya are practised today :

1. **'Vikat Lasya'** : The dance form in which Laya, Taal, Bhavas are exhibited while performing, is called 'Vikat Lasya'.

2. **'Visham Lasya'** : By using 'Bhramari' through horizontal, circular and slanted movements, special footwork in Laya based dance, 'Visham Lasya' is performed.
3. **'Laghu Lasya'** : By producing sound on earth through anklets and through Anchit Kunchit Padvinyas, 'Laghu Lasya' is performed.

In this dance, instruments with soft sound, high bass are used such as 'Manjira', 'Flute', 'Ghunghroo' (anklets), 'Madal', 'Khol', 'Tabla', 'Tumburu' etc.

The costumes used are extremely shringarik and attractive. The female dancers use Chunnatdar Dhoti, broad Waist Bandh and Patka. They also wear garlands of flowers in their hairs and Chunnis of bright and dark colours. The hands and neck are adorned with pearls and flowers.

3. HISTORY OF INDIAN DANCE

History of Indian dance form can be traced to pre Vedic period *i.e.* Indus Valley Civilization. It is revealed from a dancing figurine found in the course of excavations at Mohan Jodaro and Harappa, that dance had important place in the social life of the people of those times and they were quite well versed in this art.

Indian people had knowledge of music and dance even during 5000-6000 BC, which is acknowledged by famous historian Fedis also.

The art of dance as practised by Dravids was also of high order and from their life we learn of richness of 'homogeneity', 'vision' and 'beauty of innerself'. Dravid women were proficient in dancing and beautiful.

1. **Indian dances during Vedic period :** During the Vedic age, Indian Dance took a new turn. It was enriched with new emotions and variety of presentation. In the Vedas, which belonged to this age, the word 'Nritya' has been mentioned at various places. It is also revealed that the Rishis (Sages-learned men) of this age were well aware of the art of dancing. According to Prof. Alag Retorn, artists of all three types i.e. singers, dancers and instrument players were present during this age. Women dancers used to participate without any hesitation in public performances of music as singers, dancers and instrument players and enjoyed high status in the society. In Brahmins, Upanishads and other Vedic scriptures of this age, Nritya has been described vividly.

   We thus see that during Vedic Age, dance was an important social activity. In all festivals and functions, Nritya was an essential performance and was viewed highly.

2. **Nritya during Aryan Period :** Aryans linked Nritya to Yoga, made it simple to learn and gave it a spiritual meaning. They used practice of dance to purify and strengthen their mental

state and capabilities. Aryans believed that dance was a powerful medium for purifying the soul and taking it out of darkness and evil thoughts. They elevated their state of mind through practice of dance.

During this period, Natya Nritya (dance drama) Geet Nritya (dance and song) Roop Nritya (abhinaya and dance) Bhav Nritya (emoting through dance) were developed which enriched and elevated the level and content of dance. Aryans laid great importance on purity and considered purity as beauty. Beauty was however, considered to be mother of Nritya. Nritya was considered as an expression of beauty.

3. **Nritya during the period of Ramayana :** Nritya was fully developed during the period of Ramayana. It is known from the Valmiki Ramayana that people belonging to both high as well as lower strata of society in this period were skilled in all the three arts of music *i.e.* singing, dancing and instrument playing. Amsagie has written in his book that musical excellence of the order, the glimpse of which was found in the Ramayana age, was not found in the prior periods.

   Rama was also skilled in music, playing of instruments and painting. Ravana, the king of Lanka also used to worship Lord Shiva with song and dance and his wife Mandodari and other women of the palace were proficient in all types of arts.

   It can thus be concluded that various types of arts including singing and dancing attained significant progress and improvement during this age.

4. **Nritya during the period of Mahabharata:** During the Ramayana period, we find that all classes of society had developed interest in Nritya but the art of dancing i.e. Nritya got fully developed during the Mahabharata period. During this period, the number of dancers was very large.

   Krishna is the 'sutradhar' (around whom the entire Mahabharata developed) and he was the master of the art of dancing. He performed 'Raas Nritya' with Gopis (village women) and used to leave everyone spellbound. The great grandson of Krishna, Pradyumna and his wife Usha learnt 'Lasya' style of dancing from Goddess Parvati (wife of Lord Shiva) and then propogated it in Dwarika. Similarly, Arjuna learnt the art of dancing from Urvashi, a nymph from heaven and during the period of his banishment when Pandavas were required to live incognito, he transformed himself as Brihnnala, the Eunuch and taught the art of dancing to Uttara, the daughter of King Virat. Thus it can be seen that even the main characters of Mahabharata were quite skilled in the art of dancing.

5. **Nritya during Bauddha period:** The great war of Mahabharata led to widespread destruction. The ordinary people were scared and the art suffered gradual decline. Buddha, the knowledgeable one, in about 2500 BC, preached religious and social reforms and showed the way to Nirvana (relevation) to people.

   Buddha encouraged the male as well as female dancers to participate in social functions and when women went for darshan of Buddha, they praised him through the medium of singing and dancing. The art was also used for propogating Buddhism and bringing it closer to common folk.

   Lord Buddha, also known as Siddharth in his early life was skilled in various types of arts and artists enjoyed a status in the society. 'Amrapali' was the famous danseuse of Buddha period that ultimately became his disciple and renounced the world but this reveals that the art of dance developed significantly during this period.

6. **Nritya during 3rd Century A.D.:** In the closing stages of 3rd Century A.D., the art of dancing underwent revolutionary transformation. This was the period of 'Nagas'. It was during this age that Muni Bharat, the great master of Music, created 'Natyashastra' which is still available.

   The peculiarity of this age is that the Naga people used music and dance in the process of worshipping and they raised the art of dance as also other arts beyond the level of sensuality. They built Rangshalas (auditoriums and theatres) at various places to facilitate performances. In this age, expression of bhavas (emotions) through mudras was considered superior.

7. **Nritya during 4th Century A.D.:** Chandra Gupta II who also assumed the title of Vikramaditya, was son of Emperor Samudra Gupta and ascended the throne in the year 375 AD. During his reign considerable progress was made towards further development of fine arts like music, dance and painting. Emperor Samudra Gupta had established a strong and stable kingdom and due to advancement made by the society in various spheres of life, Gupta period has been referred as the Golden period of Indian history.

   In his book "The Essence of Indian Music", Shri BullDog Ipsa has mentioned "I consider the Gupta period as the Golden period of music only because during this period even the ordinary people had such high level of understanding of literature and fine arts which is not found even today in people who are highly educated and belong to the progressive class."

   During Gupta period, Indian music and dance crossed the frontiers and became popular in foreign countries. From the idols and paintings of this age, it can be summarized that the artists of this period had elevated dance to a form of devotion and they emoted each sentiment in the most beautiful and presentable manner.

   The great poet and playwright Kalidasa belonged to this period and his plays prove that drama, dances and music were evolved and established in their classical form. Dances were developed through plays and many famous dancers such as Malavika of Malavikagnimitram and Urvashi, main character of 'Vikramourvashiyam' a play by Kalidasa belonged to this period.

8. **Dance during Rajput period:** Rajput period extended from 687 AD to 1000 AD. Durlng this period, art forms were not practised by masses but became a profession by personal choice. Many of Idols, sculptures, paintings were destroyed by invaders. According to many experts, the tradition of

'Gharanedari' took roots during this period as artist started confining their skills to themselves. An author by the name of Ajmat has recorded in his diary that "The Rajput kings of those times loved music with the same intensity as they were brave." Many musicians found shelter in the courts of the kings and the art progressed under the protection of the kings. Women used to participate in the social festivals during this period.

9. **Dance during Moghul period:** The period beginning from the reign of Emperor Akbar and upto the end of the rule by Emperor Shahjahen is known as 'Later Middle Age'. Both the emperors were lover of fine arts. The Dhrupad and Dhamar styles of singing were born during this period and much advancement was made in dance form. It was during this age, that changes were ushered into costume of Kathak but the spirituality of Vedic age began to vanish gradually.

    To derive pleasure and entertainment from dance, Bhavas were depicted in a relatively cheap style and gradually dance came to be associated with prostitutes. The Lord was displaced by the King and renowned artistes were made to dance with a cup of wine in their hands for the enjoyment and pleasure of the kings.

    In other provinces of India, various styles of dances were, however, developed during this period. In south India, the environment for dancing continued to be classical and spiritual as it was not affected by Muslim culture. The kings in south India established dance schools and bequeathed villages to dance teachers. Various dance Mudras were sculptured on the pillars of the dance schools.

    During the period belonging to Vijaynagar Kingdom, Krishnadev Rai had set up a 'Ganika Nagar' for the dancers. The dancers used to live here as Devdasis. During this period 'Bharatnatyam', 'Kathakali', 'Kuchipudi' and 'Yakshagan' were in full bloom along with Kathak. Around the end of Moghul period, the Nawabi reign came into being in Oudh and the 'Lucknow Gharana' of Kathak was founded.

10. **Dance during European period:** The advent of the European races into India resulted into an appreciable influence of Western culture on Indian Culture. Since they had brought rich cultural traditions with them, this age can also be referred as 'Renessaince of Cultural Consciousness' as Europeans in their spare time used to listen and watch Indian music and dance and this provided an opportunity for Indian dance and music to evolve on the international scene.

    It was during this age that the music began to be taught through institutional medium due to efforts made by Pt. Vishnu Narain Bhatkhande and Pt. Vishnu Digamber Paluskar, who set up music institutions in various provinces of the country.

    In this age, literature concerning Indian music was written and many Indians as well as European scholars got attracted towards Indian music and culture and wrote books of high quality.

    This age also saw emergence of artists of international repute, notable among them were Gopinath, Reeta Devi, Ragini Devi, Shiv Shankaran Namboodari, Smt. Rukmini Devi Arundel, Meenakshi Sundaram Pillai, Smt. Bela Saraswati, Sri Ram Gopal and Sri Uday Shankar who performed overseas and made Indian classical music and dance internationally recognized. We may thus conclude that during European age, Indian dance was revitalized.

11. **Indian Dances post Independence:** The country shed the yoke of slavery on 15th August 1947, which led to popular awakening in various spheres including fine arts. As a result Indian dances became popular among masses. In major cites of the country, institutes dedicated to the teaching of dances were set up and dance was introduced as a subject in the schools and universities.

    In the post independence period, there have been considerable changes in Indian classical dance styles in regard to presentation, makeup, dress, use of musical instruments, light and sound. Many books have been written in Hindi, English and other languages on Indian dances.

In the year 1954, Sangeet Natak Academy was set up by the Central Government, which has made considerable contribution towards preservation and development of traditions concerning music, dance and drama. The academy organizes many programmes, provides financial aid to artists and honours them as well. Now Indian artists go abroad to perform.

Post independence, Indian dances have entered the homes of the common man and the art has achieved a status and recognition in the society. People belonging to all classes feel a sense of pride in learning classical dance.

Our Government has played an active role in encouraging classical dances and as a result, its future appears quite bright.

4. CLASSICAL DANCES OF INDIA

Indian dances are an ancient art form whose beginning can be traced to 'Natya Ved'. It is based on Natya ved. Bharat has explained in detail the art of dance in Natya Shastra.

Initially, the object of dance was only spiritual elevation and the performance was only to worship the God. Such dances were called 'Margi' dance. Additionally, another dance style was also common, called 'Desi' which was for public entertainment. 'Margi' and 'Desi' dances have evolved into today's classical dance forms.

Kathak Dance

KATHAK is a word of Sanskrit language and it literally means story or story teller, one who reads aloud "Puranas' *i.e.* "Kathakar" or "Kathavachak". It is from the word Katha the word 'Kathak' developed and became popular which means a caste engaged in singing, playing instruments and dancing.

Learned people have said 'One who tells story is called Kathak'. It is evident that the dance Kathak relates to story (Katha) and the tradition of the story telling is quite ancient. Instances are found in Vedas, Puranas and other scriptures *e.g.* in the court of Lord Rama, the disciples of Sage Valmiki *i.e.* Lava and Kusha narrated the story of Lord Rama by singing and enacting the same. In fact, this dance form has its origin to the period of Lord Rama. The storytellers who followed this style were called Kushilava and later on were called "Kathak'. Similarly, the story of Lord Krishna *i.e.* "Bhagvata" was narrated in the temples through songs and dances.

In the medival age, when large scale destruction of temples took place, these story tellers called 'Kathak' lost their shelter and began to scatter and found refuge in the courts of Kings or Nawabs and started creating dances according to their respective tastes and to establish themselves in the court, they innovated to create extraordinary effects.

It is also believed that in the Muslim age, Kathak had to be totally transformed. Hindu culture was destroyed and Kathaks had to absorb the court's pomp and show and sense of pleasure. In this age, Kathak style of dance emerged as a means of entertainment and sensual pleasure. In this age, Kathak style of dance emerged as a means of entertainment and sensual pleasure. In this age the "King" replaced the Lord and "Devdasis" became "Saki'. The dance imbibed Muslim literature, Ragas and Beats and poems like Ghazals. Thumri became subject of dance form. The dependence of Kathak dance on the court brought the artists (Gunijan) and the audience both closer to prostitutes as a result of which the standards of morality began to dilute. The system of "Gharanedari' also developed around this time. The three houses of Kathak *i.e.* Lucknow, Jaipur and Banares were founded.

During the declining phase of Muslim rule, Nawab Wajid Ali Shah and thereafter Nawab Rampur, Raja Chakradhar Singh etc. made their contribution to keep this dance form alive but generally during the European age, this dance form almost became extinct.

However, during last few decades, the attitude of society towards Kathak has undergone a change and with the establishment of music institutes, the image of Kathak has improved. As a result, boys and girls of cultured families were attracted to this dance form.

Kathak is the classical dance form of Northern India. In the performance of Kathak, the artists enjoy a lot of freedom, usually not available in other dance forms. Each Kathak dancer begins the dance in his or her unique way and organizes the performance according to his preference. However Kathak dance performance is usually divided in two parts: (1) Nrit and (2) emoting. Kathak begins with Nrit under which 'Thath', 'Amad', 'Tode', 'Tukde', 'Paran' and 'Tatkar' are performed. Under emoting aspect, 'GatNikas', 'Gatbhava' and 'Thumri Bhav' or 'emoting a poem' is performed. In Kathak dance, "Ghunghroos" are actually used in a unique manner. Each 'Bol' emanating from 'Tabla' and 'Pakhavaj' is matched by the dancer through the Ghunghroos. The spectacular aspect is performance of 'Bhramris'.

The costume of Kathak: Women usually wear Lehnga Choli and Dupatta while performing Kathak. Male dancers wear Churidar Paijama, Kurta and Angarkha and tie a Dupatta in the waist.

Bharat Natyam

Bharat Natyam is a popular classical dance form of South India. It is related to Devdasis. For the beautiful expression and artistic presentation of Bharat Natyam, much credit goes to Devdasis. The teachers of Bharat Natyam called Nattuvan were considered to be acharyas of this art. These Nattuvans used to train their female disciples free of charge. After training, their disciples used to earn and give a part of their earnings to their teachers.

Being naturally religious, in southern provinces Bharat Natyam was popularised by Devdasis in temples. These Devdasis could be divided into three categories :-

- Rajdasi
- Devdasi
- Swadasi

Bharat Natyam is considered famous for its spectacular speed and expressions through body movements.

The presentation of the dance can be divided into following seven sequential stages:

1. **Allaripu:** the dance begins with prayer mudra which is considered Allaripu. It is characterised by identical positioning of both sides of the body. Movement of neck, eyes, eyebrows is called 'Rechak' and movements of both sides of the body is identical.

2. **Jethiswaram:** In the second stage the dance is accompanied with singing which is called Jethiswaram.

3. **Shabdam:** In the third stage, prayer is offered to the Lord and the king is praised through poems.

4. **Varnam:** In this stage 'emoting' and 'footwork' reach their climax and the Nayika emotes some Shringaric story.

5. **Padam:** The dancer emotes on poems in this stage.

6. **Tillana:** This is the sixth stage. A spectular effect is created with rapid speed of ghunghroos and most beautiful body movements

7. **Shlokam:** By reciting shlokas in sanskrit, prayers are offered to Lord Krishna.

Costume of Bharat Natyam: The dancers wear tight dhoti (Langdar) in which an attractive dhoti with pleats is joined in the centre; which at the time of foot work spreads like peacock feathers between the legs. Patka and kamarbandh add further attraction to the costume.

Men usually wear a Patka and Kanthi (a type of necklace) while women wear choli and special garlands.

Kathakali

This dance is particularly popular in Kerala state of South India. It has a beautiful combination of music, story and emoting. In this dance form, 'emoting' has dominance. The dance features stories of Ramayana, Mahabharat or any other mythological story. The actor playing the role comes on the stage and enacts according to the story while in the back ground, musical compositions are played to explain the Bhavas.

Kathakali dance is characterised with the dominance of 'Tandava' element and Veerta (Bravery), Adbhut (spectacular) and Shant (peace) rasas are also established. The body movements are complex and the number of mudras also are many more than those found in other classical dance forms. In this style of dance, the Abhinay part is important.

The dance begins with a prayer to God sung from behind the screen. Thereafter, the instrumentalists play together and in the same beat 'Mardul' is also played alongwith which the male or female dancers come on the stage gradually and emote according to their roles through body movements. For example, if the role of Ravana is to be played then all the expressions will be that of Roudra or Bhayanak Ras (Anger). As a result the actor does not recite the dialogues like in a drama but emotes through facial expressions and body movements.

Costume of Kathakali: In this dance costume designing and make up are of great importance. Characters wear tight jacket and colourful ghaghara (long skirt) which remains blown. They also wear a crown according to the role whose halo may stretch upto their feet.

The colour of the face is according to the role. The faces of gods are green, that of demons, red or black. Women and other minor actors have natural coloured face.

The decoration and make up is according to Abhinaya.

Manipuri Dance

There is a folklore related to this dance that once when the Gopies were engaged in dancing with Krishna in 'Maharaas' the Natraj Shiva sought permission to witness the same. Krishna permitted him to watch the performance but only with his back facing the dancers but Shiva was so enchanted with the dance, sound of Mrudangs, flute and guhungroos that he forgot his promise and hiding himself watched the dance. He then returned to his abode in Himalaya and decided to perform the 'Raas' with his wife Parvati.

For performing 'Raas', Shiva chose Manipur and invented instruments like 'penga' and 'Pena'. Sheshnag (the king of serpents) lit up this area with the 'mani' in his hood and since then the region is known as 'Manipur'.

The dance having been influenced by 'Maharaas' describes mostly the playful acts of Krishna. This dance is usually performed by girls but men are not barred from performing it.

In the Manipuri dances four types of Raaslilas are performed *i.e.* Vasant Raas (Raas of spring season), Maharaas (Raas of full moon day), Kunj Raas (Raas of tree clusters) and Nitya Raas (Eternal Raas).

This dance has a preponderance of 'Lasya' and the footwork, eyebrow movements, hand gestures and body postures all imbibe 'Lasya'.

Costume: The costume of Manipuri dance is extremely, attractive and colourful. The women dancers wear a costume called 'Pulloi' A loose lehanga of bright satin or silk is worn which is called 'coomin'. It is adorned with motifs made with glass and Jari which is covered by transparent silk or peshwan. To blow the 'coomin' near the knees, bamboo sticks are placed inside in a circular form. The face of the dancer is covered with transparent silk. The hairs are raised and then tied in a knot. The shape of the knot is according to the type of Raas. The Gopis usually wear costume of red colour while Radha wears green colour.

Kuchipudi

The history of Kuchipudi dance is quite old but it was recognised as a classical dance much later. Its origin is placed around 2nd century BC. Since the dance evolved in the Kuchipudi region of Andhra Pradesh, it is known as Kuchipudi dance. It is a traditional dance drama which bears distinct influence of Vaishnav sect. This dance form is also influenced by oddissi and Bharat Natyam dance styles.

The dance is usually performed in the following manner :

(a) *Poorvarang* : This is akin to Bhoomi puja (worshipping the earth) followed by prayers to Shiva, Vinayaka or Venkateshwar.

(b) *Bhamakalapam* : This is the second stage of the dance in which the dance is performed based on a story line.

(c) *Shabdam* : The third stage of the dance is called shabdam in which a "word' is expressed by emoting in various manners.

(d) *Dashavatar* : In this stage all the ten incarnations of Lord Vishnu are described.

(e) *Rama Pattabhishek* : This is the fifth stage in which the story of Rama-right from his birth to ascendancy on the throne is described through the medium of dance.

(f) *Tillana* : This is the 6th stage in which dance is performed through "Tillana" which is pure beats and laya.

(g) *Tarangam* : Tarangam are the poems composed by

Narayan Tirtha describing the childhood acts of Lord Krishna. In the end there is spectacular exhibition of 'Layakari' and 'body movements' which is performed by the dancer while standing in a Thali (plate)

Costume:—The women wear sari and blouse and use waist band. Women also wear an ornamental belt in the waist and arm bands, tika and necklace. Men usually wear a dhoti, waistband and Dupatta.

Oddissi Dance

Oddissi is one of the oldest classical dance forms of India. It was born in the temple of Lord Jagannath in Puri in oddissa which was always the centre of art, literature and culture in the Eastern India. The dance evolved through devdasis in the temple called Mhari and the boys called 'Geeti yuwan' who danced in female dress.

It is a solo dance conforming to the roles of 'Natya Shastra' and 'Shilp Shashtra' and is performed in the following six stages :

1. The dance begins with bowing to earth and prayer to 'Vighnaraj' by singing 'Mangalacharan' and dancing on it.
2. The second stage is 'Batunritya' which initially performed at slow pace using 'Charis', 'Bhangimas' and 'Karans' and is speeded up gradually.
3. After Batunritya, prayers are offered to the Lord which are taken from Sanskrit or Oriya literature.
4. Next stage is called 'Pallavi' in which Hastaks (hand gestures) are demonstrated according to the music.
5. After 'Swar Pallavi', next stage is 'Abhinaya' which is similar to 'Padm' in Bharat Natyam or performance of Thumri in Kathak. Expression through eyes is of much importance in 'Abhinaya'
6. The performance is concluded with 'Tarjan' which is somewhat similar to Tarana of Kathak or Tillana of Bharatnatyam involving demonstration of 'Swar' 'Tal' and 'Nrit' in which, pace is continuously increased and dance reaches its climax.

Costume: The women wear silk sari with a 'Lang' whose spread hangs in the front. They wear a waistband of silver, most of the ornaments are made of silver the hairs are arranged in a round knot and adorned with buds of pearls.

Mohiniattam

According to some folklores, Lord Vishnu first performed 'Mohini' dance on the shores of Kerala and the same dance is popular in Kerala in some or other form and is known as 'Mohiniattam'. The origin of this dance form is attributed to the devdasis of Tamilnadu combining with the Nagyars of Kerala. While the dance of devdasis had a preponderance of Lasya, the Nagyars were skilled in emoting through facial expressions and combination of the two skills led to development of Mohiniattam style of dance in the temples. In this dance there is a distinct importance of court songs and music. The dance is performed in the following sequence.

First stage commences with 'Cholketu' in which the Lord is worshipped with prayers. It is followed by Taliswar Varnanam, Padm and Tillana. The dance is concluded with shlokam in a very interesting style. The shlokam are devotional in nature.

Costume: The female dancer usually wears a white sari with a broad red border. The sari is kept upto the calves. Hairs are tied into a bun on the left side above the temple and further adorned with fresh fragrant flowers.

5. FOLK DANCES OF INDIA

The tradition of folk dances is continuing from Vedic age. Folk dances of each country reflect the customs, rites and behaviour of each country.

Folk dances strengthen mutual relations and provide happiness and establish peace and harmony in the society. Folk dances are usually related to religious festivals, agricultural processes or natural or geographical conditions.

For performing folk dances, no external accessories are required. These dances can be performed anywhere and there are no set rules for them.

Folk dances reflect the ideals, thinking process, customs, rites, religion and special features of the society in a natural way.

We now give below a description of main folk dances of India:

(1) **Folk Dances of Rajasthan:** Ghumar and Jhumar are the main dances of Rajasthan. These dances are performed on important occasions and festivals. On the festival of Holi, Deepawali and Gangaur the atmosphere reverberates with Ghumar dance. In Ghumar, dance performing women wear 'Lahanga' and 'Odhni' and carry large plates full of lighted earthen lamps while moving their feet. In this dance, women move in a circle and because of this movement it is called Ghumar. Like Ghumar in Rajasthan, 'Bhawai' dance is also practised widely. 'Bhawai' is a dance of a sub-caste of Rajasthan. This is a dance of the men folk and is based upon a narrative. The narrative is particularly accompanied with song and dance. The entire dance is organized on the basis of local folklores and the performers of the dance keep on moving from place to place.

Apart from Ghumar and Jhumar, 'Dandia' 'Rasiya', 'Dhol' 'Dance of Matkas (pitchers)', 'Dance of swords', 'Dance of Snake Charmers' and 'Dances of Kalbelias' are also important dances of Rajasthan.

(2) **Folk Dances of Gujarat:** The 'Garba' dance of Gujarat has an important place in main folk dances of India. This dance represents the folklores of Gujarat. The women of Gujarat have given such prominent place to Garba that it is performed with devotion and respect on all religious occasions.

Garba begins from first day of 'Navratri' and is performed over 9 days. This dance is mostly performed by women. On the first day of 'Shukla Paksha' of Hindu month of 'Ashwin', the 'Ghat' (pitcher) for worshipping is decorated. The Garba ghat is made very beautiful and is decorated by painting flowers and leaves on it and an earthen lamp full of clarified butter (Ghee) is lit inside the ghat and then the ghat is worshipped. Women carry bedecked ghats on their heads and move in group to each other's houses. On a particular place, they set down their ghats and form a ring around ghats.

The dance group has a leader called 'Naika' who first sings a line from the song and thereafter other women repeat the same. The speed (Gati), beat (Tal) and rhythm (Laya) of this dance are not very difficult. However, the movement of the body parts is very beautiful. The group of women first bends in one direction and then other. The dancers clap while bending down to feet. The women from Gujarat weave the rise and fall (Aaroh and Avroh) of song in a rhythm and dance in a very pleasant way. Once, the dance is over, the offering (Prasad) is distributed which is called 'Salhani'. On the last day, the ghat is disposed off in river or pond or sea.

Just like Garba is a dance meant for women, the 'Garbi' dance is performed by men. This dance is also performed during Navratri for worshipping 'Mother Goddess'. In this dance, a painting of 'Mother Goddess' is placed in the centre, an earthen lamp full of clarified butter (Ghee) is lit in front of it and recently sown barley in an earthen pot is kept next to it. The dancers perform with this painting in centre and all of them wear traditional Gujarati dress.

Like Garba and Garbi dances which are extremely popular, 'Dandia Raas' is also an important dance form. In this dance, men and women, both take part. They carry small batons in their hand and they dance in small circles. While dancing, the dancer strike the baton on the baton held by the other performer and maintain continuity of the beat. These batons are usually painted with different colours and embellished with bells which produce mellifluous sound while dancing.

(3) **Folk Danes of Uttar Pradesh:** Nautanki is considered to be the most popular dance of UP and is the means of entertainment for the masses. In this dance, the story in lyrical form is narrated by the actors on the stage, who also dance simultaneously. The story is often related to the contemporary social problems or national feelings. In fact, during pre-independence period, it was used for evoking nationalist sentiments of masses.

Like Nautanki, Raasleela dance is also quite popular. Raasleela is actually a Natya (Drama) belonging to the region of Braj in which the stories of Lord Krishna and his consort, Radha, are enacted. The dance is often performed by children who dress like milk maidens (Gopi) and perform on the basis of poems composed in Brajbhasha (A variant of Hindi spoken in the region of Braj). The enactment of Raas has an important place in the culture of Braj. The stage for performing Raas is very simple and without much adornment. On the stage, a small throne is kept for Radha and Krishna and place for seating the 'Gopikas'. The front portion of the stage is used for dancing and around the stage, place is reserved for seating the musicians, singers and audiences. Before commencing Raas, the Raas troupe performs auspicious beginning by singing poems (Padas) composed by famous poets of Brajbhasha. After that, Aarti is performed and then Raas begins. Raas is charaterised mainly by singing and dancing.

Some other folk dances are also popular in UP viz. Chapeli, Thali dance, Judda and Jhenta dance, Manjari dance.

In Chapeli dance, the dancers describe the pleasant memories of the unification (Milan) and poignant moments of separation. There are no limitations on the number of dancers. The songs are usually love songs. The sensuousness and elation which is found in Chapeli dance is not available in other dance forms.

Kajri dance is also very popular in UP. With the onset of rainy season, the Kajri dance also arrives on the scene. Married daughters return to their parents from the house of in-laws to play on the swings. These swings are installed on the robust branches of the Neem tree and are swung high. When women sing mellifluously while playing on swings, the other set of women automatically start moving rhythmically along with the songs.

(4) **Folk Dances of Maharashtra:** Maharashtra is also famous for its folk dances. Some of the main dances are 'Dholacha', 'Konlyacha', 'Dadhikala or Handinritya', 'Dashavatar', 'RadhaNach' 'Tamasha' etc.

Dholacha is a folk dance full of elation and excitement. In this dance 'Dhol' instrument has an important place and as such it would be appropriate to call it 'Dhol Nritya'. In the dance, dancers stand very closely in a circle and put forward a little their left leg. They move in circle putting their hands either on each other's shoulder or around the neck or waist and call loudly "ho ho ho".

Dadhikala or HandiNritya has Krishna Leela as its theme. This dance is performed on the day following Gokulashtami. The dancers call "Govind-Govind" and go to each other's house dancing on the way. In this dance, a child plays the role of Krishna and other dancers put their hands on each other's shoulders and move forward tapping their feet on the ground in a sequential manner. A pitcher full of butter and curd is hung at some height and the boy acting as Krishna climbs on the shoulders of the dancers, reaches the pitcher and breaks it causing the curd to fall. For grabbing the curd, the dancers and audience rush in and it is believed that there would be no dearth of milk and curd by performing the dance.

Like HandiNritya, Dashavatar is also a religious dance and in this folk dance story of various reincarnations of Lord Krishna is presented. The narrator (Sutradhar) first of all prays to Lord Ganesha and Saraswati and invites them on the stage and then through them presents the various reincarnations of Lord Vishnu in their garb on the stage.

RadhaNach is also a popular dance of Maharashtra. This dance is charaterised by emoting the poems depicting the playful episodes of Lord Krishna and Radha through facial expressions. In this dance, Radha is kept in the centre and it is performed with simple body movements. To begin, the main dancer (Nayak) sings a line from the song and then other dancers repeat the same. This dance is characterised by exquisite dress and beats.

Lavani is the traditional folk dance belonging to the state of Maharashtra. It is performed for entertainment only. Lavani dance does have religious or mythological themes like in some of the other folk dances of India. Lavani can be performed either vigorously or in a soft and subtle manner. It is performed by a beautiful dancer clad in a bright nine yard saree and lovely pearl and golden jewellery. It is performed by the main dancer, her co-dancers, a person with a dholak and another person who announces the Lavani in the public. The person who announces the Lavani on stage is called "Paindya". The dance starts with the dholak wala playing the dholak vigorously and the Paindya shouting "Aaika ho Aaika" attracting the attention of the public. Aaika means 'Listen'. The main dancer enters the stage flaring the 'pallu' of her saree and then facing the audience paying them greetings known as "Mujra". Mujra is a gesture which is performed by the hand and bending towards the audience. The main part of the dance is performed on the Marathi songs which are full of life. Lavani is performed by trained dancers in the open like on a small stage on the ground or now even in the theatres.

(5) **Folk Dances of Punjab:** The way wheat crop sways on the land of Punjab, the folk dances of Punjab are also full of emotions, intensity and energy.

The chief folk dance is 'Bhangra', which is performed on occasions but begins from the sowing of the wheat. The dance is started with playing of 'Dhol' inviting the young men who gather on listening the Dhol sound. They dance in a circle moving in a circular fashion and while dancing, call "ho ho" and lob the sticks held in their hands in air and clap simultaneously. The dance starts at a slow pace but gathers momentum gradually and is performed over a long time.

Like Bhangra, Gidda is also a famous folk dance. This is a dance essentially of women performing in a group. In this dance, the women move in circles and in between move very rapidly while holding hands of other women. They also maintain the pace of the song by clapping. Gidda dance enhances the grace of functions like marriage ceremonies.

(6) **Folk Dances of Bengal:** In the folk dances of Bengal, 'Raibeshi' is foremost. This dance belongs to Domo lower caste residing in the districts of Birbhumi and Murshidabad. It is mainly performed by men folk. The dancers perform in circles and wear anklets (Ghungroos) in the right leg. No one sings in this dance and the beats of the Dhol change along with the change in gestures of the dancers.

Similarly, 'Kathi' dance is also a dance of backward castes. In this, the dancer holds small stick in each of his hands holding aloft the head and strikes one stick with the other while moving in a circular manner. In this dance, the musical instrument used is called 'Madal'.

Apart from the above two dances, 'Dhali' and 'Baul' dances are also popular in Bengal. The Dhali dance shows courage and the dancer performs while holding a shield (Dhal) in his hand. Baul dance is performed with songs rendered with the music being played on Ektara (an instrument with a single string).

The old folk dance of Bengal is 'Kirtan'. Here the playful acts of Lord Krishna are described. The dancers perform in a circle and along with the Mridung player also dances while playing Mridung. This dance is full of devotion to God.

Jatra is another famous folk dance based on playful acts of Lords Krishna. In this dance, many sensual events of Krishna's life are described.

(7) **Folk Dances of Assam:** A variety of folk dances are popular in Assam such as 'dances of Khasi tribe", 'Bodo',

'Bodokyari tribe dance', 'Bihu dance', 'Naga dance', 'Nurharalim dance' etc.

In Khasi tribal dance, the women adorn themselves by wearing a sliver crown embellished with feathers and men wear attractive turbans, hold swords and use the tail of the animal. This dance is of the maiden girls and involves specific body movements.

The Bodos or Bodokyari tribals dwell in the plains of Assam and are worshippers of lord Shiva. They depict the acts of lord Shiva in their dance. Assam is considered as the land of Nagas. Their dances relate to acts of bravery. Naga dancers wear attractive dress and adorn themselves with skins, bark, corals, conches, pearls and feathers.

(8) **Folk Dances of Bihar:** The more popular folk dances in Bihar are 'Jadur Lok Nritya' and' Santhal Lok Nritya'.

Jadur Lok Nritya is performed in the spring season and is a dance of gaiety and excitement. It is performed by both men and women. Once a movement with speed is performed by men, the women repeat the same.

The folk dance of the Santhal tribe of Bihar has its own place. It begins with the beating of Dhol and Nagaras on the full moon day. The young men sing and the girls dance.

(9) **Folk Dances of Himachal Pradesh:** Main folk dances of Himachal Pradesh are 'Banjara', 'Gaderiya', 'Ghughati', 'Lavli', 'Bangavali', 'Chauraha' etc.

Banjara and Gaderiya dances are based on folk songs. The dancer enacts the role of trader or shepherd. The dances of hills are not bound by limitations.

Ghughati dance has been named after a mountain bird of the same name. In this dance, the performers stand in a circle and start dances with the beat of the 'Dhol '. The performer also sings along with the dance.

The Lavli and Bangavali dance are also attractive dance forms. Along wlth the dancers, the audience also starts swaying. The groups of dancers put one leg forward and one backward, bend forward once and then rise and move hands in air and dance in a round circle. This dance is performed at the time of ripening of harvest or marriage.

(10) **Folk Dances of Andhra Pradesh:** Main folk dances of Andhra Pradesh are 'Dappubagham', 'Mathuri', 'Bathkampa', 'Kummi', Kulattam', 'Lambadi', 'Siddhi', 'Chenchu', 'Gadaba', 'Poroja', 'Kodh' etc.

In Dappubagham dance, a Dhol called 'Dappu' is played. Usually male Harijans participate in the dance and each dancer plays Dappu while performing.

Mathuri dance is performed by both men and women. Men and women both form separate groups. Men hold small sticks in their hand and women give them company by clapping.

Bathkampa folk dance is also considered as one of the main dances of Andhra Pradesh. It is performed by women on the occasion of marriages. In this dance, the song narrates the old story of 'Saijanbai'.

In lambadi folk dance, the women wear multicoloured dresses. It is performed in the night around fire where men and women dance together, while singing simultaneously.

(11) **Folk Dances of Tribals:** The emotional background of folk dances of tribals residing in the hilly and sub-hilly regions of Vindhyachal Mountain is similar to those of other parts of the country. These dances are full of excitement, valour and speed. Gond culture has a distinct place of its own.

Karma dance is considered to be main dance of the Gond tribe. Often men and women standing in a row sway and sing sensual song and dance. Men dance in circles playing their instruments and show their aerobatics. They dance climbing on the shoulders of others. Then they get down and sit in circles and keep on dancing in this way. As the beats of the instruments become faster the rhythm of dance also becomes faster.

The Gond youth perform another dance at the time of sowing of the crops which is called' Beyphutani' dance. Gond dance is performed to please the rain goddess to ensure enough water availability.

The dances of Bhils and Banjaras are particularly popular in the region of Central India. The 'Dagli' dance of Bhils, which is very entertaining, is performed only by men. In 'Pali' dance, both men and women join. The 'Lagi' dance of Banjaras is performed in the Hindu month of 'Shravana'. In this dance, mostly songs narrating brave deeds are sung highlighting the valour. In the songs of Banjaras, often the story of Prithviraj Chauhan is narrated. 'Ghera' dance as evident from the name itself is performed in circles. The Banjaras hold each other's hands and dance moving into the circle. The 'Lota' dance of women is very attractive. In this dance, they keep a tumbler on their heads and dance.

The dances of Banjaras in south India are slightly different but movements of body parts and Mudras (expressions) are often similar. In South India, the Banjarans can be married only if she is a skilled dancer. In their dances, many of their daily rituals are reflected. While dancing, Banjaras and Banjarans put on garland as worn by Gypsies and adorn themselves with stones. Their skirts (Ghagharas) are of either dark colours or white. Their blouses are studded with star and glass beads and are made by stitching together a number of cloth pieces. The women wear bells (Ghungroos) in their wrist and not in ankles.

The Gonds of Hyderabad dance moving from place to place. They are treated with respect in the villages which they visit. In 'Dandia' dance, they move in circles and the beats are created by striking batons. It is said that Dandia dance has been named after a person 'Dandaria'.

6. COMPARATIVE STUDY OF KATHAK DANCE AND FOLK DANCE

Folk Dance	Kathak Dance
1. In folk dances, regional dresses are used.	1. In Kathak, the dress used is according to 'Gharanas'.
2. In folk dances, simpler beats are used.	2. In Kathak dance, complex beats and rhythm are used.
3. These are based on folk lores.	3. Kathak is often performed on literary poems.
4. In folk dance, any particular Rasa (emotion) is prominent.	4. In Kathak, all the Navarasas (9 emotions) can be exhibited in a single performance.
5. Folk dances represent the diverse culture of the vast India.	5. Kathak dance mainly depict civilization of Moghul times.
6. In folk dances, only songs are used but there is no Padhant (calling of beats).	6. In Kathak dance, along with song, Padhant (calling of beats) has important place.
7. Beats (Tal) and rhythm (Laya) are important in folk dance.	7. Apart from beats and rhythm, the work of bells (Ghungroos) has special importance.
8. Folk dances are performed in a group.	8. Kathak is usually performed Solo.
9. Folk dances are performed on the ground and do not require stage.	9. Kathak requires a special stage for performance.
10. Folk dances involve traditional body movements and foot work.	10. Kathak involves classical foot work, body movement expressions (Mudras), Chakkar to create special effect and beauty.

●●●

2

1. GHARANAS OF KATHAK

Lucknow Gharana

The Lucknow Gharana of the Kathak traces its origin to Sri Ishwari Prasadji, who was the resident of the Handia Tehsil of Allahabad. Once Lord Krishna inspired Sri Ishwari Prasad in his dreams to rejuvenate Kathak dance and he dedicated his entire llfe for its cause. He had three sons: Adguji, Khadguji and Tularamji whom he trained in Kathak till the age of 100. At the age of 105, Sri Ishwari Prasadji died due to snake bite and his wife performed 'Sati' with his dead body. Influenced by this incident, Shri Tularamji renounced this world and Khadguji stopped dancing. Adguji trained his three sons: Prakashji, Dayalji and Harilalji. After the death of Adguji, Prakashji was appointed as Court dancer in the court of Nawab Asfudaullah. He also authored a book 'Pothi Prakash' which is now not available. Prakashji had three sons: Durga Prasadji, Thakur Prasadji and Manji. Manji was conferred the title of 'Singh' by the Nawab but it was Thakur Prasadji who won acclaim as dancer. Thakur Prasadji was appointed as 'Guru' of Nawab Wajid Ali Shah. Durga Prasadji had three sons: Shri Bindadinji, Shri Kalka Prasadji and Shri Bhairon Prasadji. Bindadin Maharaj and Kalka Maharaj pair was known in the Kathak world as 'Yugal' and became famous throughout the country. Bindadin Maharaj composed 1500 Thumris.

Kalka Prasad has three sons: Achhan Maharaj, Lachhu Maharaj and Shambhu Maharaj. The dance maestro Shri Birju Maharaj is the son of Shri Achhan Maharaj, who with his devotion and dedication has given a new dimension to Kathak. Shambhu Maharaj had two sons: Shri Krishna Mohan and Shri Ram Mohan, who are teaching Kathak in 'Kathak Kendra' at Delhi.

The House of Lucknow is the main Gharana of Kathak dance style. In this Gharana, the custom is to dance in small Tukdas (pieces). In these Tukdas, stress is laid on beauty of body parts. In this Gharana, 'GatNikas' is often presented. Singing of Thumri and emoting simultaneously is the specialty of this Gharana. In the Tukdas of Tatkar, 'Ta Thai Tat' are danced in many variations and 'That' is also expressed in a particular way.

The heritage of Lucknow Gharana can be written as follows:

LUCKNOW GHARANAS

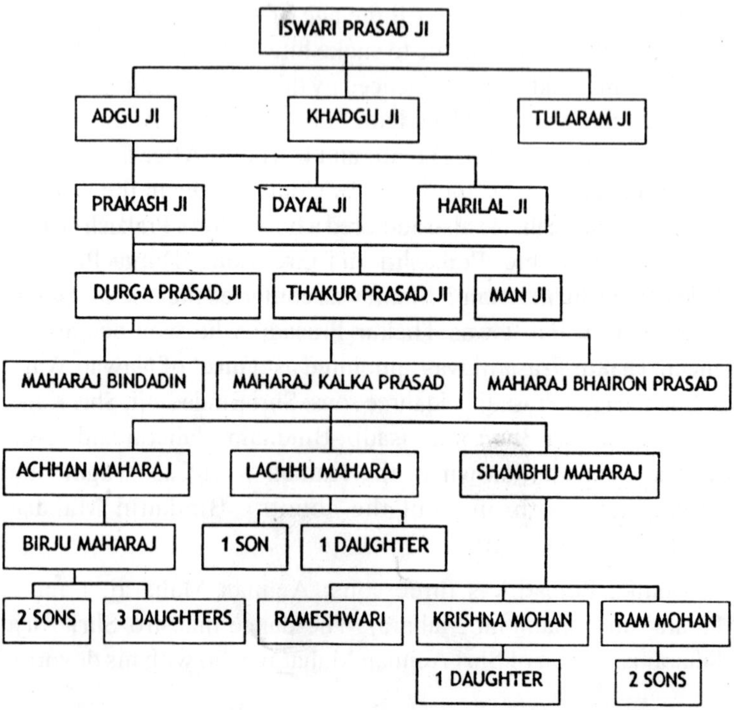

Jaipur Gharanas

Founder of Jaipur Gharana was Bhanuji, who received training in Tandava dance from some saint. Bhanuji's son was Maluji. Maluji's sons were Laluji and Kanuji, who were traditionally trained in Shiv Tandava. Kanuji went to Vrindavan and received training in Lasya and honed his skills in other styles. Kanuji had two sons: Gidhaji and Shejaji. Gidhaji had five sons, one of whom was Dulhaji. Dulhaji had two sons: Hanuman Prasad and Hariprasad. The pair of Hanuman Prasad and Hariprasad was known as 'Devpari'. Both of them were appointed in 'Gunijan Khana' of Jaipur Court. Hariprasadji was famous for Akashchari and Hanuman Prasad for Lasya Natya.

Hanuman Prasad had three sons: Mohanlal, Chiranjilal and Narayan Prasad. Narayan Prasad wrote 'Asankhya Kavitt' and Bhajans which are sung with respect in Jaipur Gharana. Narayan Prasad's sons Charan Girdhar Chand and Tej Prakash Tulsi maintained the tradition of their Gharana and are imparting training to a large number of disciples in this style of Kathak. Tej Prakash Tulsi expired some time before.

Many relatives of Hanuman Prasad and Hariprasad were also dancers viz., Shyamlal, Chunnilal, and Durgaprasad Govardhan etc. Jaipur Gharana has a number of branches out of which Shri Jailal and Shri Sunder Prasad both sons of Shri Chunnilal are particularly famous. Shri Jailal had one son Shri Ram Gopal who lived in Calcutta and trained disciples there. Jailal's daughter Jaikumari also achieved fame in Kathak dance.

The dancers of this Gharana were mostly engaged in the courts of the Hindu Kings. Because of this, many old traditions of Kathak dance are still safe with this Gharana. In this Gharana, footwork on difficult Layakaris and Bols are paid special attention but not the movements of hands. However, purity (Satvikta) of Bhav is maintained.

JAIPUR GHARANAS

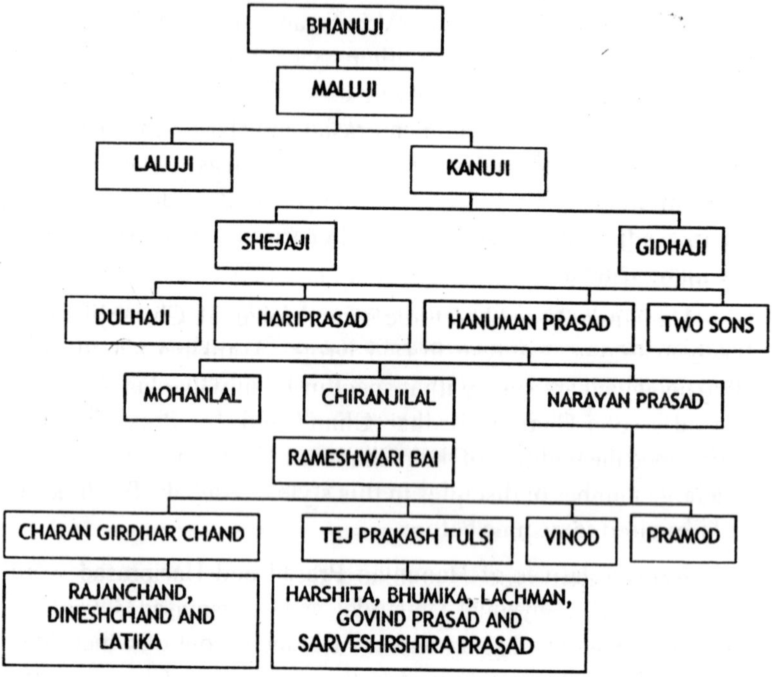

Benaras Gharanas

Benaras Gharana is also known as Janaki Prasad Gharana. He was the native of Benaras. In fact, he along with his two brothers Dulha Ram and Ganeshilal had come to Benaras from Jaipur and settled down here. It was in Benaras where his Gharana prospered. Janaki Prasad had three main disciples: Chunnilal, Dulha Ram and Ganeshilal. Chunnilal received Kathak training from Janaki Prasad for 15 years and was appointed Court dancer in Bikaner. Janaki Prasad trained his younger brother Dulha Ram. Dulha Ram trained Ganeshilal.

Dulha Ram had three sons: Biharilal, Hiralal and Puranlal. Ganeshilal also had three sons: Hanuman Prasad, Shivlal and Pt. Gopalji. They were all great dancers of their times. Hanuman Prasadji also had three sons: Nawal Kishore, Bansidhar and Omkar Prasad. Shivlal also had three sons: Sukhdev, Durga Prasad and Kundanlal. Pt. Gopalji had only one son: Krishna Kumar, who is not alive any more. Sitara Devi, daughter of Sukhdev Maharaj is the most famous exponent of this Gharana.

Janaki Prasad Gharana is based on purity of dance, Bols, purity of Bhav (Satvik Bhav) and Tatkar. In this Gharana, stress is laid on Nikasi by footwork. Whereas, others tap feet 4 times in "Tigda Din Din', in this Gharana feet are tapped 6 times. Heel is most extensively used.

BENARAS GHARANAS

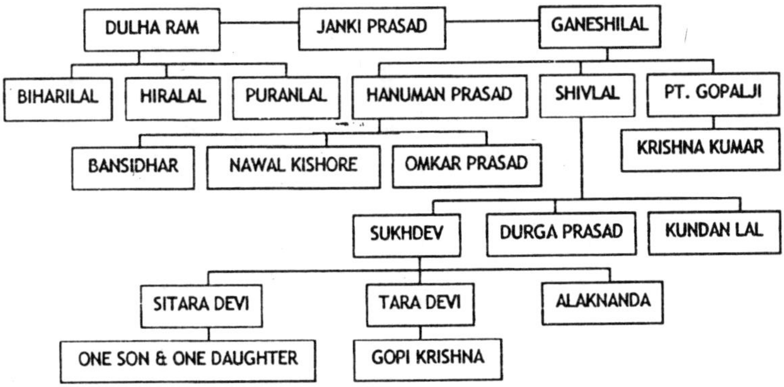

2. A COMPARATIVE STUDY OF LUCKNOW, JAIPUR AND BENARAS GHARANAS

	LUCKNOW	JAIPUR	BENARAS
1.	This Gharana had its origin at Lucknow. It prospered here.	The centre of this Gharana was Jaipur in Rajasthan.	This Gharana evolved at Benaras.
2.	This Gharana was founded by Shri Ishwari Prasadji.	This Gharana was founded by Shri Bhanuji.	This Gharana was founded by Shri Janaki Prasad.
3.	Lord Krishna had inspired Shri Ishwari Prasad in his dreams to revive the Natwari style of dance.	Shri Bhanuji was trained in Tandava style by a sage.	Janaki Prasad came to Benaras and created this new style.
4.	This Gharana was patronized by the Nawab of Oudh and Muslim rulers and hence the influence of Muslim culture is evident.	This Gharana was patronized by Hindu Kings and hence is influenced entirely by Hindu culture.	This Gharana imbibes both the Tandava and Lasya and the influence of Hindu religion is evident.
5.	`In this style, Lasya is important and depicts soft Bhavas (sentiments).	The Gharana involves special preparations in which stress is laid upon purity of footwork.	This Tandava dance characterises this Gharana and hence the spirit of bravery is reflected in this style.
6.	Thumris are more often used.	Devotion is the main theme.	Prayers of Lord Shiva and Krishna are mostly used.

7.	Use of Kavitts (Poems) is nominal. Emoting is based on singing of Thumris & Ghazals.	Kavitts (Poems) are more often used.	Kavitts (Poems) and Thumris both are equally used.
8.	Bols of Tatkar are 'Tigda Dig Dig Tigda Dig Dig'.	Bols of Tatkar are 'Ta Thai Thai Tat'.	While Bols are same as Lucknow Gharana, in Padnikasi, feet are tapped 6 times.
9.	Due to Muslim influence, the costume usually comprises Angarkha and Paijama. There is not much difference between the costume of men and women dancers.	In this Gharana, usually Bandi (Vest) and Dhoti are worn by male dancers and Lehanga and Choli by female dancers.	The male dancers wear only Dhoti and nothing above waist. Female dancers wear Lehanga and Dhoti.
10.	Bhramari is not much used.	Bhramari is more often used.	Bhramari is more often used.

3. BIOGRAPHIES OF KATHAK GURUS

Achhan Maharaj

Achhan Maharaj was born to Shri Kalka Prasad in his maternal village Lamuha Distt, Sultanpur. He was very pleasant by nature and hence was called' Achhe Bhaiya' by people. He was the eldest son of Kalka Prasad and his real name was Jagannath. He was called emperor of dance in the 20th Century and had a command on the most intricate beats while performing dance.

Alongwith beats and rhythm he was proficient in emoting. He used to show the feminine beauty and feelings through his dance and emoting which held the audience spellbound. His dances were mostly based on playful acts of Lord Krishna. He composed a number of dances which had Krishna as the theme. Apart from these dances he used to recite Thumri or any poem (sher) of urdu and then emoted the same.

He loved the city of Lucknow. He used to say that in the environs of Lucknow the Nazakat (softness of Nawabs of Lucknow) was imbibed which was as useful for dances as the mountainous environment was to the patient of Tuberculosis.

During his last days he wrote a book on the art of dancing which contained traditional (Gharandedari) items but the book was stolen due to carelessness of members of family.

Achhan Maharaj had only one son Pt. Birju Maharaj who is engaged in development of Kathak dance and imparting its training to his disciples.

Udaishankar

Udaishankar was born on 8th December, 1908 at Udaipur. The name of his father was Dr. Shyama Shankar Chowdhary who was Adviser to the Government in the Education Department of

Jhalawad (Rajasthan) and later became Dewan of the State. Udaishankar was named after the city of his birth i.e. Udaipur. Udaishankar achieved world-wide fame and is credited with introducing to the world the Indian dance styles. Since childhood Udaishankar was interested in music and painting. In the year 1917 he took admission in Sir J. J. School of Arts at Bombay and joined the Royal College of Arts London in 1920 to pursue higher education in painting. It was a coincidence he came into contact with famous Russian Baile artist, Anna Pavlova. For almost two years he remained with Anna's troupe. Thereafter, he formed his own troupe and performed Indian dances in Europe and America.

Udaishankar returned to India in 1929 and trained in Kathakali with Shankaran Namboodri and in Bharatnatyam with Khandapa Pillai. He also studied Manipuri dance and other folk dances and combining the specialties of various dance forms, invented a new style of his own. He set up an Art Centre near Almora for imparting training but it could not be seen for long.

Udaishankar experimented with shadow dancing by throwing light from behind the screen and produced a feature film 'Kalpana' but he incurred heavy loss in this venture. He, however, gained much fame at international level.

Udaishankar was awarded Fellowship of 'Rashtriya Sangeet Natak Academy' and Deshikottam by VishwaBharti University and Padma Vibhushan by Government of India.

Udaishankar will be always remembered for providing a new direction to Indian dance. His dance style is also known as Oriental style. Udaishankar, the doyen of Indian dances died in the year 1977 at Calcutta.

Kalkaprasad

Kalka Prasad born in 1842, was the son of Shri Durga Prasad and younger brother of Maharaj Bindadin. He died before Maharaj Bindadin. He is said to be extremely handsome and his dance is also said to be equally beautiful. Apart from Kathak dance he was proficient In playing Tabla and Pakhawaj. Together with his brother

Bindadin he earned name and fame in Kathak dance all over the country. The specialty of his performance was expressing the Thumri while dancing and singing it simultaneously and his way of expressing the feminine softness sensually mesmerized the audience.

Kalka Prasad lived in Benaras throughout his life. He trained the Tawaifs (Prostitutes) of Benaras in thumri singing and expressing it artistically.

Kalka Prasad had three sons—Jagannath (Achhan Maharaj), Baijnath (Lachhu Maharaj) and Shambhunath (Shambu Maharaj). All the three sons were master of Kathak dance with their own respective stamps on the dance. Kalka Prasad died in the year 1913 AD.

Kartik Ram

Kartik Ram was born in the village Bhanwarmal of Dist. Bilaspur (MP) in the year 1910. His initial training was under Pt. Shivnarayan. Later on he trained in Kathak dances under Jailal, Shambhu Maharaj and Lachhu Maharaj. He had keen interest in folk dances which enhanced the creativity of Kathak. He was a protege of the King of Raigarh who arranged for his education in music and dance for which great artists like Jailal and Achhan Maharaj were appointed.

As long as Raja Chakradhar Singh was alive there was no parallel of Kartik Ram in Taiyyari (preparation) but today very few know him.

Kartik Ram was awarded with 'Shikhar Samman' for 1980-81 by the Government of Madhya Pradesh. He also worked as Kathak dance teacher at Khairagarh and Chakradhar Nritya Kendra Bhopal.

Kundan Lal

Shri Kundan Lal was a Kathak dancer belonging to Jaipur house (Gharana) of Kathak. His education and training was imparted by his uncle Shri Narayan Prasad whom he accompanied to Raigarh. Thereafter, he travelled in Bihar and Madhya Pradesh for five years each. Afterwards, he lived in Mumbai for 15 years and taught Kathak. Many film actresses were his disciples, prominent among them were Swarnlata, Paro and Jabin. In 1953 he was appointed Kathak director in Dance department of Baroda University. He died on the 16th July, 1984.

Kumudini Lakhiya

Kumudini Lakhiya started dancing at a time when the art of dance was on a decline. She accompanied Ramgopal when he was going to Europe on a cultural tour. During this trip she earned enough fame in Europe and America.

Her dance training took place under Pt. Radhelal Mishra (Jaipur Gharana), Ashiq Hussain and Sunder Prasad. Ministry of culture gave her scholarships to enable her to receive training in Kathak dance from Shambhu Maharaj. She also worked with Birju Maharaj in 'Malti Madhav' and 'Kumar Sambhav' dance drama. Her creative talent has impressed all the artists.

In the year 1980 KumudiniLakhiya was honoured by Gujarat State Sangeet Nritya Natak Academy and Rashtriya Sangeet Natak Academy respectively. She married Rajni Lakhiya and settled down in Ahmedabad where she is imparting dance training.

Gopi Krishna

Gopi Kishna was born in the house of his maternal grandfather Shri Sukhdev Mishra. The name of her mother was Tara and renowned dancers of Kathak world, Sitaradevi and Alaknanda are his maternal aunts. His childhood was spent in Mumbai and after school education he went to Calcutta where his father trained him in Kathak.

Gopi Krishna received training in Kathak from his maternal grandfather, Shri Sukhdev Mishra and maternal uncle Chaubey. Apart from Kathak he also trained in Bharatnatyam under Govindraj Pillai.

He returned to Mumbai to begin his professional career and worked as dance director in many films. He achieved much fame for his work in the film in 'Jhanak Jhanak Payal Baje' and reached the pinnacle of glory.

Gopikrishna did not believe in blindly following the traditions. As a result he introduced some new elements in Kathak and became a dance director. He died in Mumbai in the year 1994.

Jailal

Late Pt. Jailal was a pillar of Jaipur house (Gharana) of Kathak. He was born in the year 1885. His dance training took place under his father Chunnilal and uncle Durga Prasad. Apart from being a dancer he was also a good tabla player and musician.

Jailal was also related to the courts of Jaipur, Jodhpur, Raigarh and Maihar and remained a dance teacher till the last years of his life. He had two children; a daughter, Jaikumari and a son, Ramgopal, both of whom were great dancers of their times; particularly, Jaikumari was considered as the best dancer of the country in those times.

Jailal was considered a master of beats(Tal) and Rhythm(Laya). He used to present large beats in a very simple manner and made spectacular presentation of 'Layakari', long 'Parans', 'Parmelu', 'Jati Puran', 'Pakshi Paran' besides impressive 'Padhant' which were high points of his dance. He died in the year 1949 at the age of 64 in Calcutta.

Pandit Duargalal

Pt. Durgalal was born in the year 1948 in Mahendragarh (Rajasthan). His father's name was Pt. Onkarlal. Durgalal received his dance training from his brother Devilal, Durgalal was considered to be a Jewel of Jaipur house (Gharana) of Kathak. Within a short period he created a place for himself among the Kathak teachers and dancers of the country.

Pt. Durgalal was honoured by Rajasthan Sangeet Natak Academy and Rashtriya Sangeet Natak Academy in the year 1983 and 1984 respectively. He was also honoured by Government of India who awarded him 'Padmashri'

Pt. Durgalal was a representative artist of Jaipur house (Gharana) who amazed the audience world wide with his creative talent in Kathak dance. Pt. Durgalal died on the 21st January 1990.

Damyanti Joshi

Damyanti Joshi was born on the 5th December 1928 in a Maharashtriyan Brahmin family. She started to dance in her childhood. She received her dance training initially from Shri Sitaram Prasad and Smt. Menaka.

Later on she trained under Achhan Maharaj, Lachhu Maharaj and Shambhu Maharaj. Apart from Kathak she also learnt Bharatnatyam, Kathakali and Manipuri dance.

She has presented many dance performances overseas and was a member delegate on Indian cultural delegation to China and Japan.

Damyanti Joshi is a proponent of purity of style and does not like too much of pomp and show.

Damyanti Joshi got the first prize for her dance in the dance Olympiad organised in Berlin in the year 1936. She was also honoured with Padmashri apart from awards given by Rashtriya Sangeet Natak Academy and Maharashtra Rajya Sangeet Natak Academy.

Pandit Narayan Prasad

Pt. Narayan Prasad was born in the year 1908 in the famous Hari Prasad - Hanuman Prasad Gharana of Jaipur. Pt. Hanuman Prasad was his father and Pandit Hariprasad was his elder uncle. His father and uncle started his dance training at the tender age of 8 years and at the age of 12, he gave his first public performance as a child dancer.

Pt. Narayan Prasad had equal command on Rhythm (Laya) and emoting in his dance. 'Shringar' was his speciality. Apart from being a great dancer, he was an accomplished player of 'Tabla' and 'Pakhawaj'. Pt. Narayan Prasad was a devotee of Lord Krishna and composed a number of Thumris and Poems(Kavitt) with Krishna Leela as the theme.

In the year 1957, he was honoured with the title of 'Nrityacharya' in Belgaum session of All India Gandharva Mahavidyalaya Mandal. Pt. Narayan Prasad died in the year 1958. He had six sons and of them Charan Girdharchand is a Kathak dancer as well as a teacher.

Maharaj Bindadin

Credit for developing and taking Kathak to its climax and having it established and respected as a great art goes to Maharaj Bindadin. He was born in a village of Handia District of UP. The name of his father was Durga Prasad. He had two brothers; Shri Kalka Prasad and Bhairon Prasad.

His dance training commenced under his father Shri Durga Prasad and uncle Shri Thakur Prasad at the tender age of 9 years. For nearly 4 years he continued to practice Tigda Dig Dig everyday for twelve hours.

At the age of twelve, Bindadin got an opportunity to show his skill in the court of Nawab Wazid Ali Shah. Accompanying him on Pakhawaj was renowned Kodau Singh but when he began to dance then Kodau Singh had to accept his defeat as Bindadin was better prepared. Wazid Ali Shah was extremely pleased with his performance and gave him substantial reward.

Later on, to make dance style more enchanting he gave it a new face. He organised Kathak in a classical way. He composed new dances and he developed Kathak as a distinct style by using new talents successfully.

Bindadin used to dance on odd beats in a way to mesmerize the audience with his younger brother Shri Kalka Prasad, he formed Kalka -Bindadin Duo which earned fame throughout the country. He composed nearly fifteen hundred Thumris and gave them new form of body movements according to the theme. He was a poet as well as a skilled dance teacher. His disciples carried forward his art and the tradition still continues to enrich Kathak.

Pt. Birju Maharaj

Pt. Birju Maharaj is the only son of famous Kathak dancer Achhan Maharaj of Lucknow. His full name is Brij Mohan Das. He was attracted towards the art of dance since childhood. He used to watch and remember whatever Achhan Maharaj used to teach his disciples. When his father saw his keen interest in dancing he accepted Birju Maharaj as his disciple by tying Ganda. At a very tender age Birju Maharaj gave his first performance at Deharadun which enchanted the audience. His father died when he was only ten years old. later on he received training from his uncles Late Pt. Shambu Maharaj and Late Pt. Lachu Maharaj. After sometime he joined Sangeet Bharti, a school in Delhi, as a teacher and composed many dance dramas.

Pt. Birju Maharaj has gained immense fame throughout the country. He is a born artist. He says that there is a huge difference between dancing and art of dancing. On the stage everything depends on God's grace and the blessings of the teacher. He says that he has to maintain the Laya and not fight with it.

Birju Maharaj is a talented artist. He presents Tihais with great beauty and can play a number of instruments particularly, tabla and pakhawaj. He is also adept in Thumri singing.

Apart from being an excellent dancer, he is a great teacher also. Many of his disciples have won acclaim at international level. Pt. Birju Maharaj has composed many dance dramas such as 'Phagleela' 'Govardhan leela', 'Malti Madhav' Kumar Sambhav' and 'Shan-e-Oudh' etc.

Pt. Birju Maharaj has been hounoured with a number of awards. He was awarded 'Padma Vibhushana' by Govt. of India. Some of the other awards given to him are Kalidas Puraskar by Govt. of Madhya Pradesh, 'Andhra Ratna' 'Nrtiya Churamani' and 'Soviet Land' award by the Govt. of USSR.

Pt. Birju Maharaj has two sons and three daughters. He is considered to be one of the icons of Kathak dance who have brought glory to the dance by making it popular at international level.

Raja Chakradhar Singh

Raja Chakradhar Singh of Raigarh was born in the year 1904. He dedicated his entire life to the cause of music. He was in a real sense dedicated to literature and music. He used his talent in varied literary styles such as poetry, story, novel writing and took practical interest in singing, playing Tabla, Pakhawaj and Kathak dance. To understand deeply Kathak he invited main Kathak teachers of various 'Gharanas' such as Pt. Jailal, Achhan Maharaj, Mohanlal and Narayan Prasad to his court for long periods and himself learnt dance from them.

Raja Saheb made a significant contribution in the field of Kathak. He defined various categories of 'Nayaks' and 'Nayikas' according to their features. Instead of Persian words such as 'Amad Salami' and 'Toda' he used words from Hindi and Sanskrit. He composed 'Jati Paran' 'Pakshi Paran' 'Kadakti Bigali', 'Dalbadal' etc.

For quite some time, Raigarh remained a pilgrimage for musicians of the country due to the patronage extended by Chakradhar Singh. Raja Saheb expired in the year 1948. In his memory, the State Government of Madhya Pradesh has set up 'Chakradhar Nritya Kendra' at Bhopal.

Smt. Rukmani Devi Arundel

Smt. Rukmani Devi Arundel figures prominently among those who participated actively in Indian cultural movement. It was surprising that she could work at ease and skillfully.

Born at Tanjore in South India she was naturally inclined to dancing. Her initial dance training was under famous dance exponent of South India, Pandanallur Meenakshi Sundaram Pillai. Coordination of Tal, Swar and footwork was the speciality of her dance.

In her art one could easily witness beautiful surge of emotions. Smt. Arundel had visualised dance as an important link in Indian cultural tradition. Her dances mostly reflected Indian ideals and spirituality. She was influenced by 'theosophy' and it left an impact on her art. Her life is a story of courage. Despite all opposition she married Dr. Arundel.

Smt. Arundel was chairman of International Academy of Arts and was honoured with 'Padmabhushan' by Government of India.

Ramgopal

Ramgopal was born in 1917 at Raigarh. He is the only son of Pt. Jailal. He was trained in dance by his father and Shri Sohanlal. He also learned Kathakali from Kunjkurup and Bharatnatyam from Meenakshi Sundaram Pillai.

Ramgopal was a fortunate person when compared to many other dancers. He went on a world tour with 'La Mera' and was well received by the audience. He also gave performances in a number of music conferences in India and displayed his artistry. With the kind of zeal and dedication, Ramgopal exploited his talent, and provided the right direction to his art.

Ramgopal was living permanently in London and running an institute. He recently died in London in the year 2003.

Rohini Bhate

Rohini Bhate started learning Kathak in the year 1946. Her initial training was under Shri Sohanlal of Jaipur Gharana. Thereafter she received training under Shri Mannalal of Mumbai and Shri Mohan Rao Kalyanpurkar of Lucknow.

In 1952 she visited China as a member of Indian cultural delegation. She has refined her technique by studying deeply old scriptures relating to Indian dances and drama. She has composed a number of dance dramas in Kathak style. She has written a number of articles on the subject of dance and two books in Marathi.

She practised Kathak hard for years and performed under the direction of Lachhu Maharaj and Mohanrao Karyanpurkar and settled down in Poona.

In the year 1977, Rashtriya Sangeet Natak Academy honoured her for creative work done in the field of dance. She has also received Kalidas Samman in the year 2001.

Lachhu Maharaj

Lachhu Maharaj's real name is Baijnath Prasad. He was the second son of Shri Kalka Prasad, the famous Kathak artist and younger brother of Bindadin Maharaj. He received training in Kathak from his father, Kalka Prasad, uncle Bindadin Maharaj and elder brother, Achhan Maharaj. He started giving performances when he was only ten years old.

Lachhu Maharaj, in the course of his performances, used to display, delicacy, sentimentality, discipline, sensuality in such a manner that it mesmerised the audience and won their uninhibited praise. He always tried to bring purity in his dances. He was in the forefront of choreography of Kathak dance in films. He easily got assignments to direct dances in the films and he successfully choraographed dances in films like Swarup Mahal, Kale Badal, Ghar Ki Laj, Shikwa, Mugal-E-Azam, Pakeeza etc. which won him immense fame in the film world.

Lachhu Maharaj also composed some special dances viz Bhartiya Kisan, Madya Nishedh etc. which turned out to be quite popular. He had knowledge of many classical dances other than Kathak also. He died in the year 1977 in Lucknow.

Shambhoo Maharaj

The name Shambhoo Maharaj occupies its own space in Kathak world. He was the youngest son of Shri Kalka Prasad. He was trained in Kathak at a tender age of 8 years by his uncle Bindadin Maharaj and later on under his elder brother Achhan Maharaj. He learnt 'Natwari' dance from Achhan Maharaj and Thumri from Ustad Rahimuddin Khan of Benaras.

Shambhoo Maharaj was known as King of emoting. According to him dance should be based upon emotions otherwise it remains only as a spectacular performance.

Apart from dance, Shambhoo Maharaj had the knowledge of Indian Classical Music. He had equal proficiency in both music and dance. He was recipient of many honours 'Such as 'Nritya

Samrat', 'Abhinaya Chakrávarti', 'Padmashri' and Academy award.

He had two sons, Shri Krishna Mohan and Shri Ram Mohan who are trying to preserve his legacy.

Sitara Devi

Sitara Devi is the daughter of Pt. Sukhdev Mishra who was a musician in the Court of King of Nepal. Her mother Matsya Kumari was the daughter of Rajguru of Nepalese Court. She had two sisters, Alaknanda and Tara.

Sitara Devi received training in dance form her father and Shambhoo Maharaj. Sukhdev Maharaj requested Achhan Maharaj also to train his daughters. Later on Sitara Devi learnt 'Lasya' from Lachhu Maharaj.

Sitara Devi learnt Bharatnatyam and Manipuri dance also apart from Kathak. This apart, she had interest in Western dances also.

Sitara had a natural interest in becoming a film actress also. In her times, she was a successful actress in the film world.

She has made new experiments in Kathak. She was honoured by Sangeet Natak Academy, Government of Uttar Pradesh and Government of Maharashtra in the year 1974. Indira Kala Sangeet University conferred an honorary doctorate on her in the year 1978. Gurudev Ravindra Nath Tagore was so impressed with Sitara Devi that he titled her "Queen of Kathak dance'. Once she danced non-stop for thirteen hours and set a record.

Sitara Devi went on tours abroad and left a deep impression of Indian dance on millions of audience. She has brought fame to the Benaras Gharana through her efforts and excellence.

Sitara Devi's first marriage was with K. Asif, second with Shri Barot, an engineer. From the second marriage she has a son. She also adopted the daughters of her brother (Mala & Priyamala) and trained them in dance. Sitara Devi's contribution to Kathak has been invaluable.

Sunder Prasad

Shri Sunder Prasad was a famous and learned dancer form Jaipur Gharana. His father's name was Chunnilal and Pt. Jailal was his elder brother.

Sunder Prasad learnt dancing from his father Chunilal and uncle Durga Prasad. He also trained under Bindadin Maharaj of Lucknow Gharana. Thus within some time he created a new style imbibing the peculiarities of both Lucknow and Jaipur Gharanas. He performed all over the country. Sunder Prasad was not only an artist but a skilled teacher also. He taught dancing for almost thirty years in Mumbai and shifted to Chennai thereafter. He was honoured by Natak Academy of Delhi in the year 1958.

Shiv Shankaran Namboodri

Shri Shiv Shankaran Namboodri was most famous of modern Acharyas of Kathkali style of dance. He was born in a high caste Brahmin family. In his time, music and dance were considered to be a vocation for lower caste but he was so much devoted to dancing that facing the opposition of his family he worked and trained hard for 15 years to learn Kathkali dance. Thereafter he formed a troupe and gave performances all over Malabar.

In 1924 Shiv Shankaran met Udaishankar who was greatly influenced by his knowledge and made him his Guru.

He travelled all over the country and overseas along with Udaishankar and contributed significantly to development and popularisation of Kathkali style of dancing.

Shivshankaran Namboodri died in the year 1943. He contributed significantly in modernising the sequence of presentation of Kathkali.

4. WESTERN DANCES

Western dances, unlike Indian dance forms which are considered thousands of years old, are considered only about 400 years old. Prior to this period, these existed only as rural dances.

The origin of western dance forms is traced to 15th Century in Italy but these attained a classical form only in France. Western dances can be considered as a gift from France. In the western world modernity is worshipped and innovation is the order.

Western dances can be classified into two categories i.e. group dances like Ball Room dance and solos and the other category being that of Baile and Operas.

Ball Room dance

Ball Room dance is quite popular in western countries and is performed by men and women. The dance is considered appropriate for men and women of all ages. For this dance, the floor is required to be flat and smooth so that during the dance, shoes may slide easily.

In this dance each pair faces each other and the left hand of the lady is placed on the right shoulder of the man and the right hand of the man is placed on the waist of the woman. Left hand of the man and right hand of the woman is placed in square shape parallel to the shoulder. In this dance only the lower portion of the body is moved i.e. the dance performed only by moving feet. The beats are created by the sole of the shoes.

Ballet/Baile

Baile entered on the scene of western dance around the ninth decade of 14th century and it developed before the world war II. This dance form owes its development largely to France and then during this century significant progress was made in USA. During this period a famous Baile dancer 'Ruthcent Dennis' made innovation in the story line of his Baile and transformed it.

'Baile' word originated from the word 'Baillere' of Italian which means 'to perform dance'. When some story is to be presented either in part or as a whole through the medium of dance then it is called dance drama or Baile.

Baile means a dance presented in a group by joining dances in a sequential manner. The performance takes almost as much time as a drama.

Opera (Geetinatya)

Opera is the art in which any play is enacted in musical form playing a number of instruments. In opera style of dance while singing the story is narrated through emoting (abhinaya).

Opera dance is created by artists from various spheres together such as Poet, music composer, singer, actor, architect decorator, instrument player, dress designer, light and sound expert, set designers, director and producer etc.

For opera first of all a story is written and it is suitably transformed into a shape suitable for music composition and singing. Thereafter, the music director composes the music for the story and the architect and decorator design the Opera House. Thereafter, the producer, director and musicians work for a longer period with the chorus singers, dancers and instrument players before presentation of opera.

In the opera entire story is presented through songs. This has two styles (a) pantomine acting—without speaking (b) vocal—speaking while acting. With the evolution in fine arts, there have been changes in opera as well. Opera dance has gained special importance as religious and social stories have been presented which has been appreciated by every class of the society.

5. MODERN DANCES

When an artist uses his imagination to create a new dance style, it is called a modern dance. Modern dances are away from classical dance but usually evolved through a combination of a number of dances. Apart from classical and folk dances, all other dance styles usually seen are called modern dances. In India, modern dances are attributed to Pt. Udayshankar & Shri Rabindranath Tagore.

Oriental dance: Oriental dances trace their beginning to Pt. Udayshankar. He studied the sculpture in ancient caves and temples, the expressions of idols and used them with mythological stories to create oriental dance and gave performance in India and overseas of this new dance style. He used to compose the dance first and the appropriate music was created for the same.

The dance did not have any restrictions on 'Tal' and 'Laya'. It was first popularised in Bengal and then all over India.

Dance Drama (Nritya Natika): The dance drama style was also initiated by Pt. Udayshankar. In this style of dance any story is presented on the stage through the medium of dance. Pt. Udayshankar provided the language of dance to ancient and modern stories and added such features which enhanced aesthetic sense of the dance.

In this way Udayshankar ended the slow paced oriental dance and composed new Dance dramas (Bailes). The name dance drama is based on western Baile and therefore dance dramas are often called Baile in India.

Modern dance dramas are enacted through rhythmic expressions. It is gradually being accepted in all classical dance forms also mainly because solo dances satisfy few spectators.

Geeti Natya or Sangeetika (Operas)

The drama in which all dialogues are in lyrical form and

characters themselves sing and emote is called Geeti natya or Sangeetika.

In evolving Sangeetika, significant contributions have been made by artists like Shanti Vardhan, Gulvardhan, Rukmini Devi Arundal, Birju Maharaj and Uma Sharma.

Rabindranath Tagore was a great supporter of this dance style and based on Rabindra sangeet he created new compositions which became popular in India and abroad.

India has its own tradition of musical dramas such as Geet Govind by Jaidev, Bhagat of Mathura and Agra, Swang of Hathras, Rahas of Lucknow and song of Haryana which is also categorised under music.

This operatic style could not develop much mainly because such actors are few who are good singers and also have acting talent.

Bhav Nritya

Bhav Nritya does not have classical complexity and only the poem is required to be emoted through Mudras (expressions). In this dance foot work is not regulated and being easy, such dances became quite popular. These dances are usually based on poems relating to nature, patriotism and gods and goddesses. Indian dances such as Garba, Shikari Nritya, Sword dances, Mayur (peacock) dance, gagri (ewer) dance come under this dance style. Classical dances have also contributed to popularisation of Bhav nritya.

FILMI DANCES: The invasion of western culture in India did influence our arts and culture and gradually Indian culture started reflecting in some way western culture also. With the mixing of two cultures, a new dance style came into being which is called 'Film Dance' or 'Record dance'.

After some time when classical dancers also entered In films, then the standard of film dance also improved. The actresses who were well versed in classical dances were quite a few, notable among them being Sitara Devi, Vyjayanthi Mala, Sandhya, Asha Parekh, Lalita, Padmini, Ragini, Hema Malini, Waheeda Rehman etc.

However, times have changed and classical music and dances have been replaced in films by loud music and dance directors choreographed such dances. Today in films a new style of music is in vogue which combines Indian & Western music and new compositions are being created. The aim of 'film dance' is only to create excitement. It has entered every house and is causing a great deal of harm to classical music and dance.

MODERN DANCES AND COSTUME : Modern dances are a mix of many dance styles and use varied types of costumes. It is usually said that the costume should reflect the surroundings i.e. the costume should suit the dance.

The costume for oriental dance is usually a dhoti or Maratha or Rajasthani style for males and for women it is usually the costume worn for Bharatnatyam dance. Men usually remain bare above the waist.

TAGORE DANCE : In Tagore dance, women wear sarees in Bangla style. In film dances the costumes have changed with the times. Initially, it was saree, churidar, paijama and kurta and odhni and later on sharara and garara but later on producers used dazzling costumes and western dresses of various types.

●●●

3

1. CATEGORIES OF NAYAKS (HEROES) AND NAYIKAS (HEROINES)

The nature of human beings differs from each other and every one behaves according to his nature. This difference in nature of human being leads to categorisation of Nayakas and Nayikas according to their respective nature. During the course of dance, the dancer acts as a narrator and displays various emotions (Rasas) for which he plays a particular character. This 'Karak' is considered under 'Vibhav' in Bharatnatyashastra. 'Rasa' emerges easily through a character. Thus the dancer must have knowledge about various types of Nayaks and Nayikas.

According to character, Nayak and Nayikas can be categorised into innumerable types but the learned writers have tried to categorise them broadly according to character, age, position and dharma.

1. **Nayak types**—According to nature nayaks could be of four types:
   (a) **Dhirodatt**—The Nayak who is polite, has knowledge about himself, is sober in nature, kind, has self respect, forgiving in nature is called Dhirodatt viz., Rama, Buddha, etc.
   (b) **Dhiroddhat**—The Nayak who is fraudulent, nimble, proud, egoist, ill-tempered is called Dhiroddhat such as Ravana, Kansa, etc.
   (c) **Dhir Lalit**—Extremely mild tempered, having sense of humour, sweet talking, fond of music and dance, is called Dhir Lalit.

(d) **Dheer Prashant**—The Nayak who is peace loving, kindly and grateful is classified as Dheer Prashant

2. On lines of dharma, the Nayak can be classified under 3 categories *i.e.* Pati, Up-pati and Vaishik.

   (i) **Pati also has 5 sub categories :**

      (a) **Anbhigya** (Ignorant)—one who is unaware of sensual acts.

      (b) **Dakshin**—one who maintains equal love for many wives

      (c) **Anukul**—one who is devoted to his wife.

      (d) **Shath**—one who ignores his own wife for another woman

   (ii) **Up-pati**—The Nayak who is involved with woman of another person is called up-pati. Up-pati has two sub-categories.

      (a) **Vachan Chatur**—The up-pati who accomplishes his goal through the gift of gab is called Vachan Chatur.

      (b) **Kriya chatur**—The Nayak who accomplishes his goal through acts of deceit is called Kriya Chatur.

   (iii) **Vaishik**—The Nayak who is involved with prostitutes, fearless and shameless is called Vaishik.

3. According to status Nayaks could be classified under two categories.

   (a) **Mani**—Unhappy on account of being insulted by Nayika

   (b) **Proshit**—The Nayak who is separated from Nayika and is consequently dejected is called a 'Proshit Nayak'.

Classification of Nayikas

Nayika is the women who invokes romantic thoughts in the heart of beholder. Classification of Nayika is based on dharma, age, nature, caste and form.

1. According to Dharma

(i) **Swakiya**—The chaste women who has love for her

husband, has made modesty her ornament, has no desire for other person even in her dreams and remains engaged in household work is called Swakiya Nayika such as Sita, Sati Anusuiyya, etc. There are three sub-categories of Swakiya Nayika.

(a) **Mugdha**—She is the Nayika who has just experienced the first flush of youth, who is shy at heart and as such hesitates and feels shy in Rati (desire)

(b) **Madhya**—This Nayika has in her heart modesty and desire both in equal measure.

(c) **Pragalbha or Praudha**—She has little modesty but is adept in the art of sex, who feels the desire in her body and soul always and who is not satisfied despite remaining in sex day and night.

(ii) **Parkiya Nayika**—The women who is secretly in love with a person other than her husband is called Parkiya. It has two sub-categories:

(a) **Udha**—The married women who does not love her husband and has a.clandestine love affair with another person is called Udha Nayika.

(b) **Anudha**—The women who is in love with another person prior to her marriage is called Anudha Nayika.

(iii) **Ganika or Samnya**—The Nayika whose chief objective is to earn and amass wealth by selling her beauty and youth is called Ganika or Samanya. It has two sub-categories:

(a) **Janani Adhini**—The Ganika who is under control of her mother and engages in trading herself is called Janani Adhina

(b) **Swatantra**—The ganika who is independent and engages in flesh trade by herself is called Swantantra.

2. **Nayika according to age**—The Nayikas are divided into three categories according to their age.

(i) **Mugdha Nayika**—Unmarried, teenaged, beautiful Nayika is Mugdha Nayika. It has two categories:

(a) **Agnyat Yuavana**—The Nayika who is unware of arrival of her youth is called Agnyat Yuvarna.

(b) **Gnyat Yuavana**—The Nayika who knows that she is youthful is called Gnyat Yuvana.

(ii) Madhya Nayika—The Nayika who has attained full youth and the feeling of shyness is not so strong is called Madhya Nayika. It has three categories:

(a) **Madhya Dhira Nayika**—The Nayika who expresses her anger on seeing the signs of sex play on her husband's body but does not abandon her respect for him, is called Madhya dhira.

(b) **Madhyaadhira Dhira Nayika**—The Nayika who expresses her anger and speaks in a pungent manner on seeing the signs of other woman on the body of Nayak is called Madhyaadhira dhira Nayika.

(c) **Madhya adhira Nayika**—The Nayika who immediately becomes angry on seeing the signs of other woman on the body of her husband and scolds him in different ways through cruel words is called Madhya adhira Nayika.

(iii) **Pragalbha Nayika**—The Nayika who becomes adult and is skilled in the art of sex, remains always unsatisfied is called Pragalbha Nayikas. It has three sub-categories:

(a) **Pragalbhadhira**—The Nayika who remains unconcerned despite seeing the signs of other women on the body of her husband but does not abandon the respect for her husband is called Pragalbha dhira Nayika.

(b) **Pragalbhaadhira dhira**—On seeing the signs of other women on the body of her husband, this Nayika expresses her ire skillfully.

(c) **Pragalbha adhira Nayika**—This Nayika on seeing the signs of other woman on the body of Nayak goes to extent of attacking him.

3. **According to Nature**—The Nayikas are divided into three categories according to nature.
   (a) **Uttama**—The Nayika who always behaves according to her husband and does not act against his interest even if he does and hides his defects, called Uttama Nayika.
   (b) **Madhyama**—The Nayika who gets somewhat angry on seeing the defects in her beloved and speaks in a harsh manner and feels sad is called Madhyama Nayika.
   (c) **Adhama**—She behaves in a manner adverse to her husband, is selfish, cross-natured, insults and agonises her husband is called Adhama.
4. Nayika according to caste: Nayikas are divided into four categories according to caste:
   (a) **Padmini**—She is born beautiful, delicate, has few hairs on body and is skilled in music and dance.
   (b) **Chitrini**—This Nayika has good character but is less shy, has interest in music and dance and is playful. She is strange natured.
   (c) **Shankhini**—This Nayika has counch shaped neck, is shameless and bitter spoken,
   (d) **Hastini**—The women who has a huge body is quarrelsome, iresome and walks like an elephant is called Hastini Nayika
5. **Nayikas according to form**—Nayikas are divided into three categories according to form :
   (a) **Divya**—This Nayika has godly qualities.
   (b) **Adivya**—This Nayika has humane qualities.
   (c) **Divyadivya**—This Nayika after being born in this world acquires godly qualities and is called Divyadivya.

2. ASHTA NAYIKA OR AVASTHAGAT NAYIKA

Eight Nayikas

At the time of Bhava demonstration in Kathak through Thumari or Kavitt, the roles of Nayikas are performed of which the Ashta Nayikas are the main. Some scholars have considered two additional categories of Nayikas *i.e.* Pravatsyanpatika and Agatpatika. Including these, ten categories of Nayikas may be considered.

1. **Proshit patika**—The Nayika whose husband has gone to a distant land and she is aggrieved due to separation, does not adorn herself, is called Proshitpatika. These are also of five types such as Mugdha, Madhya, Proudha, Parkiya and Samanya.
2. **Khandita**—The Nayika, whose husband has an affair with another woman and the Nayika knows about it, is called Khandita.
3. **Kalahantirita**—The Nayika, who first insults her husband and then repents after he goes away, is called Kalahantirita.
4. **Vipralabdha**—Nayika whose lover does not arrive at the place of meeting and the resultant anguish makes her sad is called Vipralabdha.
5. **Utkanthita**—The Nayika who for the purpose of meeting her lover reaches the indicated place but becomes anxious while waiting for his arrival is called Utkanthita or Virahotkanthita.
6. **Vasaksajja**—The Nayika who for welcoming her lover in a well provided place with all the material for the purpose of meeting, shows keenness for conjugal relationship is called Vasaksajja.
7. **Swadhinpatika**—The Nayika whose husband remains under her control due to her skill in sex is called Swadhinpatika.

8. **Abhisarika**—The Nayika, who under the spell of cupid discards modesty and either calls the Nayak or goes herself to the appointed place is called Abhisarika.
9. **Pravatsyatpatika**—The Nayika, who becomes sad on hearing the news of departure of her husband to a distant land is called Pravatsyatpatika.
10. **Aagatpatika**—The Nayika whose heart is filled with pleasure upon return of her husband from stay in distant land is called Aagat Patika.

3. MUDRAS

The word 'Mudra' is a derivative from 'Mud' Dhatu of sanskrit language which literally means pleasure. In vedas, mudra means indicating through hands. To depict various sentiments, a particular posture of body is adopted which is called 'Mudra' in dance. Mudra is very important in dance and it is called the language of dance.

'Mudras' are described in the scripture called 'Tantrasar' in which use of composite mudras by Yogis, Siddhas, Sculptors and Bauddhas has been described. Mudras can be classified into following two categories on the basis of movement of hands:—

1. **Non-Composite Mudras**—Mudras made by using only one hand; these have 28 sub-categories.

2. **Composite Mudras**—The mudras made by using both hands; these have 23 sub-categories.

Hand Gestures: Single Hand

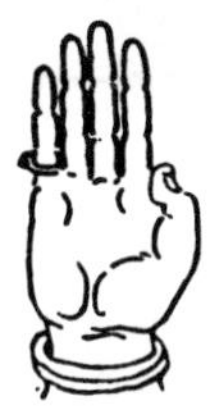

1. **Pataka Hast**—The open palm is held outward facing, the four fingers and thumb are held close together. It is used in dance to represent blessing, sleep, a river, waves, a promise etc.

2. **Tripataka Hast**—The palm face is held outwards. The thumb, first and second and little finger are kept straight. The third finger is bent into the palm. It is used to demonstrate crown, lamp, fire, tree, vajra, Indra, etc.

3. **Ardhapataka Hast**—The hand is rested with the palm facing outwards. The first and second fingers are extended straight and the third and the little finger are bent into the palm. It is used to demonstrate leaf, knife, etc.

4. **Ardhasuchi Hast**—The palm is raised outward. The second, third and little fingers are bent into the palm. The first finger is extended and the thumb is held close to the edge of the palm up to the first finger. It is used to demonstrate a bird, sprout and counting one.

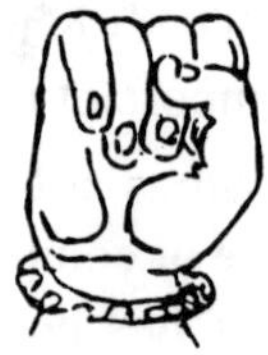

5. **Mushti Hast**—Depicts the four fingers bent into the palm and the thumb set on them. It is used to demonstrate catching of hair, holding of objects, attack, bravery etc.

6. **Shikhar Hast**—The palm is raised outwards. The four fingers are bent into the palm and the thumb is extended straight out. It is used to show belt, cupid, teeth, pillar, silence, questioning etc.

7. **Chandrakala Hast**—The palm is raised facing outwards. The 2nd, 3rd and little fingers are bent facing forward parallel to the palm and the first finger and the thumb are stretched apart and extended straight. It is used to express the crown of lord shiva, the crescent moon, the face etc.

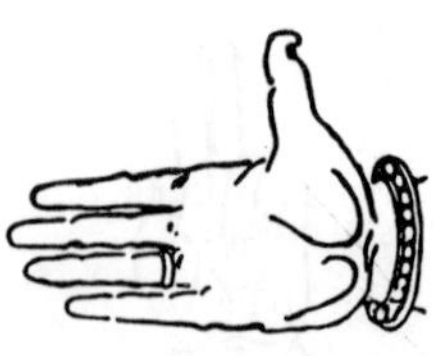

8. **Ardhachandra Hast**—The palm faces upward slightly. All fingers are stretched together and the thumb is stretched to its fullest at right angles to the rest of the fingers. It is used to show anxiety, bangle, spear, bow etc.

9. **Kartarimukha Hast**—The hand is raised with the palm facing outwards. The 1st, 2nd and little fingers are extended straight up, the 3rd finger is bent into the palm and the thumb is placed to touch the tip at the 3rd finger. It is used to show opposition, death, separation of lovers, crying, sleeping alone etc.

10. **Mayur Hast**—The hand is raised with the palm outwards. The 1st, 2nd and little fingers are extended straight; the 3rd finger is bent. It is used to show stroking of hair, the peacock, the forehead mark, etc.

11. **Aral Hast**—The palm is raised and faces outward. The 2nd, 3rd and little fingers are stretched straight. The 1st finger is crooked or curved and the thumb is a little bent beside it and almost touching the tip of the finger. It is used to express drinking poison, benediction or elixir, dressing the hair, tempest, etc.

12. **Hasasya Hast**—The palm is raised facing outward and very slightly hallowed. The little finger is extended straight. The 3rd finger is also extended but is bent slightly and the 1st and 2nd fingers are bent forward to touch the thumb at the tips. It is used to demonstrate tyings the marriage thread, certainty, making up of the painting, carrying garlands, etc.

13. **Kapith Hasta**—The palm is raised outwards. The 2nd, 3rd and little fingers are bent into the palm and the 1st finger is bent forward and the thumb is bent to touch the tip of the 1st finger. It is used to express goddess Laxmi, goddess Saraswati, garland of flowers, etc.

14. **Tamrchud Hasta**—The palm is raised facing outwards. The 3rd and the little fingers are bent into the palm. The 1st finger is bent and touches its own base, the 2nd finger is bent forward and the thumb goes to touch it at the first joint. It is used to show a camel, a cock, cart, the numbers of trees, etc.

15. **Katkamukh Hast**—The palm is raised outwards. The 3rd and little finger are extended and bent very slightly, the 1st finger and thumb are curved forward to touch at the tips and the 2nd finger is bent to touch the base at the thumb. It is used to show picking of flowers, holding of a fan, etc.

16. **Suchimukh Hast**—The palm is raised outwards. The 3rd and little fingers are bent very slightly, the 1st finger is stretched straight and the 2nd finger is bent to touch the tip of the thumb and the thumb is bent a little forward. It is used to express a saying 'this or that', Sun, body, beating of the drum, etc.

17. **Shuktund Hast**—The palm is raised facing outwards. The 1st and 3rd fingers are stretched and the 2rd and little fingers are curved forward, while the thumb is bent a little beside them. It is used to express shooting of an arrow, anger, bow, homesick mind, etc.

18. **Mukul Hast**—The palm is raised facing outwards. The four fingers are bent forward together and the thumb bent to touch the tip of the fingers. It is used to show food, Kamdev, worship, fruit, navel, etc.

19. **Padmakosh Hast**—The palm is hallowed and faces outwards. The four fingers are bent. A part of the little finger and the thumb is moved towards the bent fingers. It is used to express the bell, ball, bull, circle, etc.

20. **Al Padam Hast**—The palm is faced upwards and hallowed. All the fingers are spread out and bent to form a petalled circle. It is used to express a full-blown lotus, mandar, round face, full moon, mirror, etc.

21. **Sandansha Hast**—The palm is raised facing outwards. The 1st finger is bent down to touch the thumb at the tip and the other three fingers are extended forward and very slightly bent at the joints. It is used to show the number of fire, small bud, sprout, worship, wound, etc.

22. **Vyaghra/Urnam Hast**—The palm is raised facing downward and hallowed. All the fingers are spread out and bent except the little finger and the thumb, which are held crooked and held parallel to the fingers. It is used to express monkeys, tortoise, lion, frog, oyster shell etc.

23. **Kaungool Hast**—The palm is raised facing outwards and all but the little finger touch at the tip. The little finger is bent inward and touches the base of the thumb. It is used to express Jackfruit, white lotus, etc.

24. **Sarpashirsha Hast**—The palm is hallowed slightly, raised and faces outwards. The fingers and the thumb are close together and extended as the hood of the snake. It is used to express a snake, short man, shoulders, crown, sandal, etc.

25. **Mrig Shirsha Hast**—The palm is raised facing outwards. The little finger is extended straight, the other fingers are bent parallel to the base of the palm and the thumb is bent slightly backward behind the 1st finger. It is used to express a woman, the face of a deer, pressing of the feet, wheel of a vehicle, etc.

26. **Singhmukh Hast**—The palm is raised facing outwards. The 1st and little fingers are stretched straight; the 2nd and 3rd fingers are bent parallel to the palm and the thumb touches their tips. It is used to express a lotus garland, a yagna, etc.

27. **Hanspaksha Hast**—The palm is raised facing outward and very slightly hallowed. The finger is extended straight and the other 3 fingers are bent a little forward, while the thumb bends over to touch the center of the 2nd finger on the inside. It is used to express the covering of earthern pot, making of a bridge, etc.

28. **Chatur Hast**—The palm is faced outwards and hallowed. The 1st, 2nd and 3rd fingers and the thumb are bent like a hooded snake and the little finger is extended straight. It is used to express the face, sweetness, sorrow, kasturi, gold, etc.

COMBINED HAND MUDRAS

1. **Anjali Hast**—The palms are kept open and two hands are joined in mudra palm to palm with the fingers and thumb extended and held close together. Fingers of both hands touch each other face to face. It is used to express god, head, face and teacher, etc.

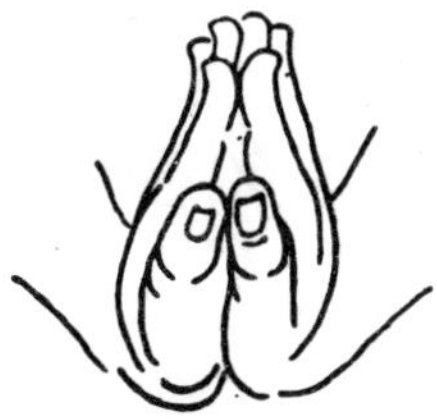

2. **Kapot Hast**—The palms of the two hands are slightly hallowed facing toward oneself and are joined at the side and the top. The little fingers touch along their sides. All fingers are extended and slightly bent. It is used to express taking of oath, politeness, acceptance, etc.

3. **Karkata Hast**—The fingers of the two hands are clasped with each other and the hands are kept with the knuckles facing outwards. It is used to express a group, arrival, blowing of conch, pressing of stomach, etc.

4. **Swastika Hast**—Two Pataka hands are crossed at the wrists where the bases of the palms touch and the left hand is placed above the right i.e. the right hand with fingers and thumb stretched are held close together pointing upwards, and the left hand with fingers and thumb in the same way also pointing up and crossed at the wrists with the left hand on the right hand. It is used to express crocodile, etc.

5. **Dola Hast**—Two Patakas are used in this. That is the hand with the fingers and thumbs stretched are placed with the back of the palms resting on the thighs. The right hand is placed on the right thigh and left on the left thigh. It is used to show the beginning of the dance.

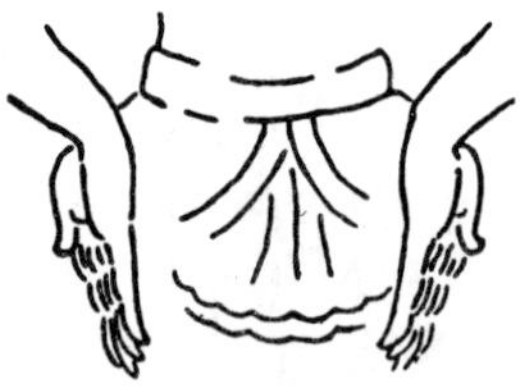

6. **Pusupaput Hasta**—The palms are hallowed slightly and face one another, fingers and thumb close together, and slightly bent at the top, the finger tips and bases of the palm in each hand are placed to touch each other. It is used to show receipt of fruits or water, giving or taking, etc.

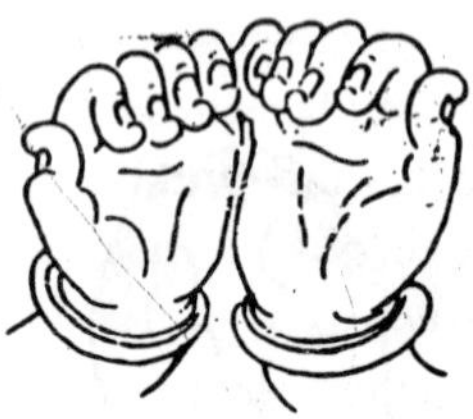

7. **Utsang Hasta**—The palm is raised facing outwards and three fingers are bent towards the palms and the thumb is bent slightly backwards. In this case, the hands are held to touch the opposite shoulders at the fingertips. The little finger is extended in both the hands. It is used to show embracing, shame, teaching the children, etc.

8. **Shivling Hasta**—Here is a combination of the Ardhachandra with the left hand and Shikhara with the right hand. It is used to express the Shiva Lingam.

9. **Katakavardhan Hasta**—The palms are raised outward and extended and bent to touch the base of the thumb. The 2nd fingers and thumbs are curved forward to touch the tips. The 1st finger is also curved forward parallel to the 2nd finger. The hands are crossed at the wrists with the hands slightly thrown back and facing in the opposite direction. It is used to express blessings, worshipping of gods and goddesses, crowning of the king, etc.

10. **Kartari Swastika Hast**—In this mudra, there is combined use of the Kartari mukha hands. The hands are crossed raising palms facing outwards. It is used to show trees, branches, the peak of a mountain, etc.

11. **Shakat Hast**—The palms are raised. The 2nd, 3rd and little fingers are stretched straight and the 1st fingers are bent and curved in half to touch the thumb and the thumbs are slightly bent outwards to touch each other. It is used to describe demons.

12. **Shankh Hast**—In this mudra, there is combined use of the Shikhara Hast. It is used to show a conch.

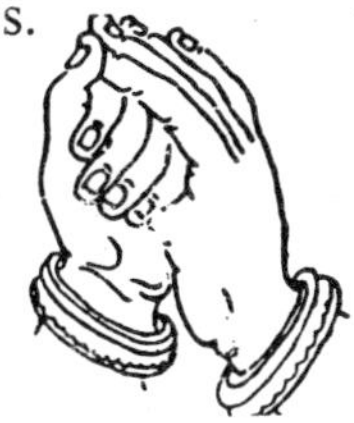

13. **Chakra Hast**—Here there is combined use of the Pataka hand slightly modified as if to clap. It is used to express chakra.

14. **Samputa Hast**—Here there is a slight deviation and modification of the Chakra Hast. It is the same as Chakra Hast except that the 1st, 2nd and the 3rd fingers are slightly bent instead of being stretched straight. It is used to show a box, a lid, etc.

15. **Matsya Hast**—The open palm of the right hand faces outward and the four fingers and the thumb are extended but the thumb instead of being placed beside the other fingers as in Pataka is spread apart. The left hand with the palm facing down is placed over the right hand so that the fingers of each hand point in the same direction. It is used to show a fish.

16. **Kurm Hast**—The hands are clasped together with the palms touching and the 1st, 2nd and 3rd fingers of each hand are bent over to touch the back of the other hand. The thumbs and the little fingers are stretched. It is used to show the tortoise.

17. **Paash Hast**—The 2nd, 3rd and little fingers are bent into the palm and the 1st finger is bent and interlaced with the 1st finger of the other. In the other hand, 2nd finger is slightly bent and the 3rd and 4th fingers are bent into the palm. It is used to express enemity or a chain.

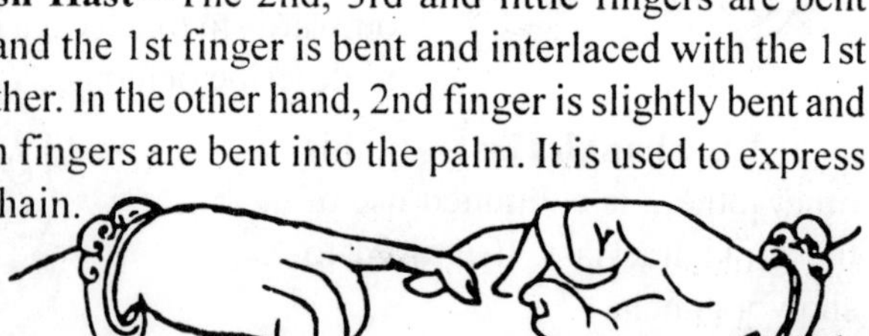

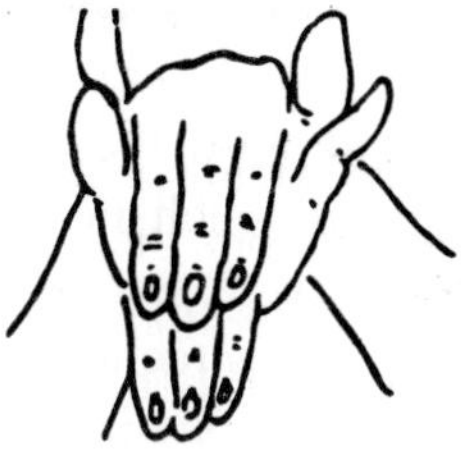

18. **Khatwa Hast**—The open palms are held facing outwards, the 1st, 2nd and 3rd fingers and the thumb are held closely together and the little fingers are stretched straight downwards. The hands are slowly moved to and fro with grace at the elbows. It shows a swing.

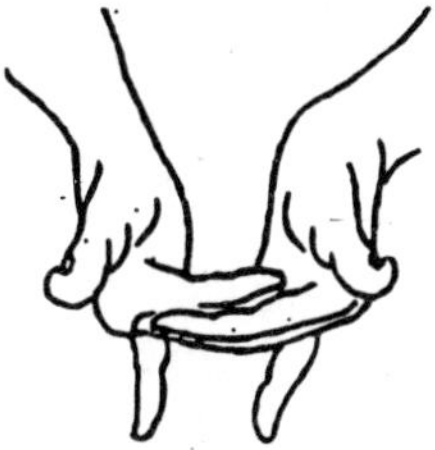

19. **Varaah Hast**—The palms are bent down. 1st, 2nd and 3rd fingers of one hand overlap 2nd, 3rd and 4th finger of the other hand. The thumbs are stretched outwards. The little fingers are extended straight. It is used to show a pig.

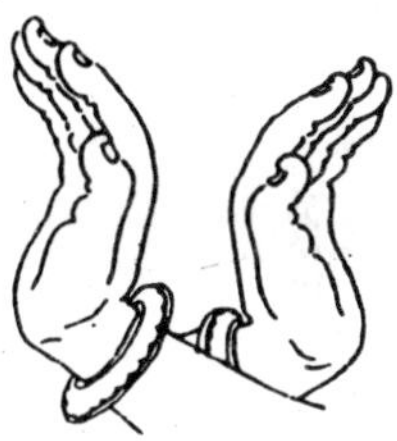

20. **Naag Bandh Hast**—In this mudra, there is combined use of the Sarpa Shirsha hand. The palm is slightly hallowed and faces outwards. The four fingers and thumb are extended close together like the hood of a snake. These hands are crossed at the wrists. It is used to show call of a snake.

21. **Garud Hast**—The hands are raised with palms facing outwards. The four fingers are stretched and the thumbs are extended away from the rest of the fingers. The hands are then crossed at the wrists and the thumbs are interlocked. The palms of the hands face inwards. It is used to show the Eagle.

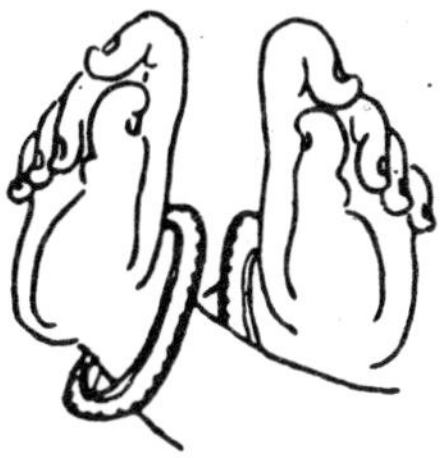

22. **Bherund Hasta**—Similar to Bhramara except that the first and little fingers are bent and come closer to the thumb. It is used to express the pair of birds, love, affection, etc.

23. **Kilak Hast**—The palms are raised. The little fingers are extended straight with the 1st, 2nd and 3rd fingertips touch the center of the palm. Hands are crossed at the wrists facing in opposite directions and the extended little fingers are interlocked. It is used to show lovers talk, affection, etc.

4. RASA AND BHAVA

Bhava is extremely important in dance. Without Bhava dance is meaningless. The thought that occurs in a person on observing/hearing/knowing any object/person/etc is called Bhava. Bhava gives rise to Rasa.

The enjoyment obtained from poetry, drama and fine arts is called Rasa.

"Rasayete aswadte iti soh Raso"

On consuming food items, the pleasure obtained from its taste is similar to the pleasure obtained from the taste (feeling) of Bhavas of many types. This is the realisability of Rasa.

The sage Bharat has described eight types of Rasas *i.e.*

Shringarhasya Karun Roudra Veer Bhayanakah
Veebhatsadbhutau chetyabtau Natyarasah Smritah

Shringar (Sensuality), Hasya (laughter) Karun (pity) Roudra (anger) Veer (Bravery) Bhayanak (terrible) Veebhatsa (hateful) and Adbhut (Strange) are the eight Rasas. Some learned persons have added shanta (peace) also as one Rasa making a total of nine.

The dancers originate Rasa through Bhavas and therefore Rasas have been considered subordinate to Bhavas. The mental state of human being is called Bhava. The artist who is able to produce this mental state swiftly is considered as competent. Each Rasa is associated with a sthayee (permanent) Bhava.

RASA	BHAVA
Shringar	**Rati (Sex)**
Hasya	**Hasya (Laughter)**
Karun	**Shoka (Grief)**
Roudra	**Krodh (Anger)**
Veer	**Utsah (Excitement)**
Bhayanak	**Bhaya (Fear)**

Veebhatsa	**Ghrina (Hatred)**
Adbhut	**Vismaya (surprise)**
Shant	**Nirved (Tranquility)**

1. **Shringar**—It is of two types (a) Sanyog Shringar (b) Viyog Shringar. Its sthayee Bhav is Rati which in larger context can be interpreted as affection or love.

(a) *Sanyog Shringar*—Wherever hero-heroine involved with each other express their love in conversation and upon seeing each other, it is called Sanyog Shringar.

(b) *Viyog Shringar*—When despite extreme affection, there is no meeting with the beloved, it is called Viyog Shringar.

(c) *Alamban*—Meeting with or separation from the beloved or achievement of desired object.

(d) *Vaibhav*—To embellish oneself, application of Sandal, desired food, not to act in an opposite manner.

(e) *Anubhav*—Smile, to point towards etc.

Following Kavitt is full of Shringar Rasa and is nibaddh in teen taal

Dekhi Roop Lochan Lalchane **X**	**Harkhe Janu Nij Nidhi Pahichane** **2**
Thake Nayan Raghupati Chabi Dekhi **0**	**Palkan hun par hari nimekhi** **3**

2. **Hasya Rasa**—When upon seeing or hearing any person/object/scene one laughs/feel like laughing it is called Hasya Rasa. The Sthayee bhava of this Rasa is Hasya.

(a) *Alamban*—Laughable Shringar, posture, act of foolishness.

(b) *Vibhav*—To ape a person, itching on the neck etc.

(c) *Anubhav*—To make faces, twisting of body parts, jumping in an awkward manner etc. Following poetry is full of Hasya Rasa

Magan Bhayee Hanse Nagar Mahesh Thadhe
Aur Hanse Aiu Hans Hans Ka Umah Mein

Sees par Ganga Hanse Bhunjani Bhujanga Hanse
Haas mein hi Danga Bhayo Nanga Ke Vivah Mein

3. **Karun Rasa**—If grief is caused by seeing a character or scene, the feeling is called Karun Rasa. Its Sthayee Bhava is Shoka (grief)

(a) *Alamban*—Death, loss of wealth, fall, injury etc.

(b) *Vibhav*—To become sorry and thrash hands and feet, feeling of sorrow, repentance

(c) *Anubhav*—Loss of voice, falling on ground, numbness etc.

Following is the example of Karun Rasa—

Priya Mrityu Ka Apriya Maha, Samvad Pakar Vish Bhara
Chitrasth Si, Nirjeev Si, Ho Rah Gai Hat Uttara
Samgyan Rahit Tatkal hi, Phir wo dhara par gir padi
Us samaya Murcha bhi aho, hitkar hui usko badi

4. **Roudra Rasa**—When on account of insult, opposition, the anger in the heart intensifies and acquires the form of Rasa, it is called Roudra Rasa. The Rasa is extremely useful for Tandava. Its Sthayee Bhava is Krodh (anger)

(a) *Alamban*—Enemy, traitor, ill behaved, ill spoken.

(b) *Vibhav*—to arrest the enemy, quarrel, fight, to reply to opposition.

(c) *Anubhav*—blowing of nostrils, sighing, raising of eye brows to bite the lips.

Following is the example of this Rasa—

Vari Tari darau Kumbh Karnahi Vidari Daron
Marau Megh Nadain Aaj Youn bala anant haun
Kahai Padmakar Trikutahi Ki thahi Daraun
Daran Karei Chatu Ghanan Ki Ant Haun
Jari Daraun Lankahi Ujari Daraun Upwan
Phari Daraun Ravan Ki To Main Hanumant Haun.

5. **Veer Rasa**—When upon seeing a character or scene the feeling of courage emanates in the heart it is called Veer Rasa. Its Sthayee Bhava is utsah.

(a) *Alamban*—Breaking of bow by Rama, seating of Rama and Lakshman by Hanuman on his shoulder, lifting of wheel by Krishna to kill Bheeshma etc.

(b) *Vibhav*—Absence of sorrow, chivalry, strength, patience etc.

(c) *Anubhav*—Stability, patience, shrewdness, pride etc.

Following is the example—

Aiso bajrangi Veer Baaji Gaj Rajan Kau
Mardan Karat Ran Mati ko so del hai
Tal Taru Bhudhar Ukhari sel Gada Kari
Ravan Ki Sain Par Karat Relpel hai

6. **Bhayanak Rasa**—When upon seeing an object or scene fear is generated in the heart, the feeling is called Bhayanak Rasa. Its Sthayee Bhav is Bhaya (fear)

(a) *Alamban*—Facing a beast, reaching in a strange position.

(b) *Vibhav*—Deep anxiety, empty house, darkness, catching electric current

(c) *Anubhav*—Trembling hand and feet, numbness, dryness of mouth, running away weeping

Following is the example—

Ek our ajgarhi lakhi, ek our mrugrai
Vikal Batohi Beeya hi, paryo murcha khai

7. **Veebhatsa Rasa**—When upon seeing any object, person or scene a feeling of hatred is created and it is called Veebhatsa Rasa. Its Sthayee bhava is Ghrina (hatred),

(a) *Alamban*—Aftermath of war where mutilated bodies are lying. Place full of stench.

(b) *Vibhav*—Flesh pieces, stinking objects, drinking of blood

(c) *Anubhav*—To turn the face in disgust, contract the nose.

Following is the example—

Sir pe baithyo Kaag, Aankh Dou Shwan Nikarat
Khaichat Jeebhhin Syar, Abihi Anand Ur Dharat
Geedh Jangh Ko Khodin - Khodin Main, Mans Ukharat
Swan Anguriya Kati - Kati Kai Khan Biyarat

8. Adbhut Rasa—When upon seeing any person, object or scene, there is a feeling of surprise, it is called Adbhut Rasa. Its Sthayee bhava is Vismaya (surprise)

(a) *Alamban*—to see an object which causes surprise, to see gods, bearing of a mountain by Hanumanji

(b) *Vibhav*—Strange object, supernatural character etc.

(c) *Anubhav*—Widening of eyes, still eyelids, flowing of tears etc.

Following is the example—

Makhan ke Chor Madhuchor Dadhichor Doodhchor
Dekhat hi Dekhat hi hiyo Hari Let Hain
Purash Puran Aur Puran Puran inhe
Purush Puran se Kahat Kihin het Hain
Kesodas Dekhi Dekhi Suran Ki Sundari Vai
Karti Vichar Sab Sumit Samet hai
Dekhi Geet Gopika Ki Bhumi Jat Nij Gati
Agatin Kaise Dhou Param Gati Det Hai

9. **Shant Rasa**—When upon seeing a person/object/scene a sense of peace or tranquility is created that feeling is called Shanta Rasa. Its. Sthayee bhava is 'Nirved'.

(a) *Alamban*—Knowledge of immortality, knowledge of God etc.

(b) *Vibhav*—Holy place, hermitage, Teertha, Dead Person, Crematorium etc.

(c) *Anubhav*—Downcast eyes, vision of Brahma, etc.

Following is the example—

Gyan det Dhyan det Atam Biyari det
Brahma Ki Batai det Brahma Mein Chatur hain
Sundar Kahat Jag Sant Kachu let Nahin

5. RASA NISHPATTI

Principles of Achievement of Rasa

It is desirable to first understand the achievement of Rasa before understanding its principles. The word 'Rasa' is made from dhatu 'Aswadan' *i.e.* taste—Rasasyate Aswadyate Iti Sah Rasa. Just like a human being derives pleasure from eating many types of food items prepared in a pure way and tasting various Rasas such as sweet etc., in the same manner by emoting various Bhavas, expression through words and body parts and Satva i.e. all the four types of Abhinaya, the audience tastes the Sthyaee Bhava and feels pleasure. This is the tastability (Aswadanshilta) of Rasa. To draw a parallel it is seen that physical Rasa is felt by various senses but the Natya Rasa can be tasted only by heart. It is a matter of heart and not of tongue. Rasa has been accepted as the last and highest goal of total performance. With the combined use of singing, instrument playing and dance, Rasa is achieved on the stage and it creates a situation in which the artist and audience both get immersed in Rasa and dip into the ocean of pleasure.

Achievement of Rasa is the feeling of pleasure. Achievement means origination. While watching a drama how the feeling of Rasa originates has been a point of debate among the learned persons.

The Sage Bharat had expressed his opinion as under :

Vibharanubhav Vyabhichari Samyogadrasmishpathi— This means that Rasa is achieved through the combination of Vibhav, Anubhava and Sanchari Bhava. The use of words Samyog and Nishpathi in this sutra has led to enunciation of various principles of Rasa by the learned persons. The principle of origin by Bhatt Lollat. According to Lollat Bhat the word 'Nishpathi' has three meanings utpatti (origin), Abhivyakthi (expression) and Pushti (confirmation). Principally there is no difference between the three like the word 'Sherbet' implies water sugar and spices at the same time.

In the context of drama Lollat said that the Sthayee Bhava resides in the drama. According to him, the audience supposes in the main and other actors of the person(s) who are being imitated. Thus Rasa first originates in the actor and it is achieved or realised by the audience but they can not feel its origination. For achievement of Rasa one requires capacity to taste (asvadan) as this is possible only when the audience has this capacity.

Principle of Imagination by Shankul—Shankul has explained 'Nishpatti' as imagination. However, mere imagination can not enable realisation of Rasa. For this it is necessary to show how the Sthayee Bhava residing in the other translates in the form of Rasa in the audience. A solution to this basic problem has been presented by Bhatt Nayak.

Bhatt Navak—Bhatt Nayak has analysed the word 'Nishpatti' according to Sankhya Darshan. He has interpreted 'Nishpatti' as salvation. Bhatt Nayak assumed the position of Sthayee Bhava in audience. According to Sankhya Darshan there are three types of Gun—Rajogun, Tamogun and Satogun. Out of these, in the state of generalisation Rajogun and Tamogun both cease their existence.

Abhibnav Gupta—Abhinav Gupta established expressionism on the basis of Shaiva Darshan. According to him the word 'Nishpatti' means expression and drama expresses the Sthayee Bhava residing in the audience and does not originate any new Bhava.

The views of Sage Muni on the principles of achievement of Rasa are more clear. He accepts the combination of Vibhav, Anubhav and Vyabhichari bhav for achievement of Rasa. In this context it is necessary to understand clearly that the word Vyabhichari Bhav does not mean dirty Bhava as understood in the popular context of today. In the times of Bharat the word Vyabhichari conveyed differently. These bhavas used to be charansheel and therefore being capable of movement. Bharat called them Vyabhichari or Charansheel Bhava. The other important aspect is that in the context of Rasa, Bharat did not use the word

Bhava directly but used a modification of this word. In this transformation he added Pralyayas and Upsargs to the word bhava and used them as Vibhav, Anubhav, Vyabhichari Bhav, Sthayee Bhavas and Satvik Bhava. Bharat Muni had special reason for not using the word Bhava directly.

The Sage Bharat while defining Bhava stated—Atmanuma Bhava Vibhav Pardarshanam *i.e.* whatever the soul feels is Bhava. The Soul or Atma is inexpressible. By seeing a beggar on the road, thousands of spectators feel in their heart a sense of pity. Pity is a feeling of soul which is called 'Anubhuti' which is an abstract feeling. Bharat considers this originally 'Bhava' when he combines Bhava with visual art then knowing that 'Bhava' is abstract, he modifies the form of Bhava and calls it Vibhav, Anubhav, Vyabhichari bhavas, Sthayee bhava and Satvik Bhava.

The principle of achievement of Rasa as propounded by Sage Bharat was analysed and reanalysed over thousands of years in the scriptures. Every learned person defined it in his own manner but the analysis made by Dr. Brajvallabh Mishra is on the lines of Sage Bharat. He confirms his views based on the statements of Sage Bharat so easily that it leaves no doubts in the minds of readers. Dr. Mishra has relied upon the word 'Tatra' in this context which has been used in the beginning of Sutra by Muni Bharat.

'Tatra Vibhavanubhava Vyabhichari Samyogadras Nishpathi'. According to Dr. Mishra till now the critics have formed their views without considering the word 'Tatra'. The meaning of word 'Tatra' is stage and with the combination of Vibhav Anubhav and Vyabhicarhi Bhavas on the stage, Rasa is achieved.

Sthayee Bhava—Sthayee Bhava is considered as the feeling in the heart of author in the course of writing. It is considered that whenever the writer decides to write a Bhava is born in his heart and that is merely an 'Anubhuti'. When he expresses his' Anubhuti' then the Bhava of 'Anubhti' achieves permanency. Even with the change of time, place and culture, the Bhav remains permanent in that composition.

Alamban-Vibhav—Nayak and Nayikas have been kept under Alamban Vibhav. Because of mutual love the Nayika becomes alamban of Nayak and Nayak becomes alamban of Nayika.

Uddipan Vibhav—Apart from Nayak and Nayika, the surroundings and their beauty becomes the cause of Uddipan (excitement) which causes feeling of Rati (sensuality) in the hearts of both viz the effect of seasons, the grandeur of forests, beautiful flowers, moonlit night, the bank of a river, breeze, music, sound of cuckoo, thunder of clouds; these are considered Uddipan Vibhav because all of them cause rising of feelings in the heart of actor. Acharya Bharat did not discuss 'alamban' and 'uddipan' alongwith Vibhav.

Vibhav—Before presenting any composition on the stage, the artist has to imbibe the underlying Bhavas and unless he does so, he can not present the performance successfully. This aspect of imbibing the underlying Bhava in the heart before hand has been called Vibhav by Sage Bharat.

Anubhav—When the heart of the artist gets affected by any Bhava he tries to follow it. The Bhavas which activate this process of following the Bhava are called Anubhav. When the tendency to follow develops on account of influence of Bhava, the state of artist is called Anubhav. Bharat Muni has related Anubhav with Bhava which inspires following up.

Satvik Bhava—Satva means 'Manovikar' the thought in the heart. In other words Satva means intention of heart. From this point Satvik Bhava means Bhavas originating in the heart. In reality it is peculiar state of the heart.

Bharat Muni did not want the artist to act only bodily but relates it to the cooperation of mind as well. Accordingly, he has provided the hypothesis of 'Satvik' Abhinaya and without accepting the dominance of Bhavas in the principles of realisation of Rasa, he has listed eight types of Satvik Bhavas e.g. sweating, thrill, pale face, trembling, fainting etc. These are the types of Bhavas which can't be demonstrated without involvement of mind.

Thus the basis for principles of achievement of Rasa as propounded by Bharat Muni are not only external but also internal, not only physical but also psychological.

Acharya Bharat Muni thus tells about eight Sthyaee Bhavas, eight Satvik Bhava and thirty three Vyabhichari Bhavas in his principles of achievement of Rasas. He considered the thirty three Vyabhichari Bhavas 'Charansheel' and these do not remain still on the face of the actor. He had defined the achievement of Rasa in the context of visual poetry.

Acharya Bharat Muni used to expect from the artist that when he performed on the stage then he should combine heart with the body. With this aim he directed the artist that before coming on the stage he should imbibe in his heart the Sthayee Bhav of original composition. It therefore can be said that Bharat Muni's principle of achievement of Rasa is the transformation of Sukshma (abstract) into Sthool (actual) the artistic presentation of Nirakar (shapeless) into Sakar (shapely). It is not a play of words but an intense psychological accomplishment.

6. ABHINAYA

Abhinaya can be defined as enacting of various stages of the character through body, heart and speech. The enactment of various stages of character of Rama, Yudhisthir, etc on stage through body, heart and speech by the 'Nat' is Abhinaya. From this point of view Abhinaya is generally perceived as 'acting' or 'copying'.

It is mentioned in Natya Shastra that "through the comprehensive use of which, the audience or spectators enjoy in their hearts the various meaning of Natya (drama) is called Abhinaya". In the Natya Shastra of Acharya Bharat following four types of Abhinaya have been mentioned.

(a) Aangik (b) Vachik (c) Aharya (d) Satvik

The four types of Abhinya mentioned above were created by none other than Natraj Lord Shankar. Acharya Nandikeshwar has mentioned in the opening Mangal Shloka of his Abhinaya Darpan that the four types of Abhinaya are four forms of Natraj. This whole universe is his Aangik Abhinaya, entire literature is his Vachik Abhinaya and this entire sky embellished with stars and moon is his Aharya Abhinaya and he himself is Satvik Abhinaya.

In the forthcoming paragraphs four types of Abhinaya are described in detail.

1. Aangik Abhinaya—Aangik Abhinaya means various actions, gestures of various body parts, limbs etc. In Natya Shastra following three types of Aangik Abhinaya have been described.

(a) *Shariraj,* (b) *Mukhaj* and (c) *Cheshtagat*

Main parts of the body are head, hand, feet, waist, sides, etc. and the Abhinaya through various postures (Mudras) and gestures of these is called Shariraj. Under 'Face' various other sub parts such as eyebrows, eyes, ears, lips, cheeks, chin, etc are included and abhinaya through various gestures and postures (Mudras) is called Mukhaj. It is in the same way the internal Bhavas are exhibited through entire body under 'Chestagat Abhinaya' for example the role of lame person, a pigmy, etc.

Acharya Bharat has narrated three means of Aangik Abhinaya.

(i) *Ang*—In Natya Shastra as well as Abhinaya Darpan both, 6 body parts for Aangik have been mentioned i.e. Head, both hands, chest, both sides, waist and feet.

(ii) *Pratyang*—Acharya Bharat and Nandikeshwar, both have classified Pratyang into a number of parts such as both hands, both arms, back, stomach, both thighs, both urus. Some of the Acharyas have included elbows, both knees and neck also into Pratyang.

(iii) *Upang*—Acharya Bharat has mentioned six upangs of Aangik Abhinaya in the following manner:

(1) Head, (2), Hand, (3) Heart, (4) Sides, (5) Waist, (6) Feet.

Harmonious and simultaneous movement of various angs in Aangik Abhinaya gives rise to activity which is called Gati Prachar. Under Gati Prachar all activities of character right from entry on the stage to exit are covered. The entry of character on the stage should be made in such a manner that there could be origination of desired Rasa in the heart of audience. In Aangik Abhinaya the body adopts a number of gestures according to the changing circumstances. The Acharya have considered four types of gestures (Bhangimas) *i.e.* Abhang, Samabhang, Tribhang and Alibhang.

In Abhang the body remains in its natural condition. In samabhang, the body remains inclined to one side. When any character stands on the stage and his body gets slightly slanted at two places it is called Tribhang and when the circumstances lead to longer bend in other parts of the body it is called Atibhang Mudra.

It is the considered opinion of Indian Acharyas that in the display of Aangik Abhinaya, the beauty of body should also be revealed for which it is necessary that the performer maintains good health since only then he would be able to have full control on his body parts and move according to his role. It is, therefore, necessary that the artist possesses healthy body and mind.

2. Vachik Abhinaya—In the tradition of Natya Shastra, Vachik Abhinaya has an important place like Aangik Abhinaya. In Natya Shastra rules have been prescribed for Yati, Kaku, Naam, Agnyat, Nipat, Upsarg, Samas, Tadhit and Sandhi. According to Acharya Nandikeshwar the dance in which the poetry and drama etc. are expressed through speech is called Vachik

Abhinaya—The definition makes it clear that the chief aim of Vachik Abhinaya is in many uses/experiments of speech. In Natya Shastra while classifying the dialects of various provinces and regions according to types of languages, it is mentioned that in the Natya the languages of four castes i.e. Barhar, Andhra, Dravid and Kirat should not be used.

Apart from the rules relating to languages and dialects, Acharya Bharat has specially considered the use of 'Reading' (Pathan), Telling (Kathan) and dialogue (Samvad) in Vachik Abhinaya. He has described six angs of Pathya (Reading material) i.e. Swar, Sthan, Kak, Alankar and Ang Shringar. Further, while delineating the use of nine rasas and seven swars he has mentioned three positions of speech i.e. heart (ur), throat (kanth) and head (shir). For this, it is necessary to know that at which place which type of speech should be used and to know about it knowledge of Swar (Tone) and Sthan (place) is essential. Proper use of Kak *i.e.* good tone (suswar) has been specially examined. From the consideration of Bhava how every performer should properly use Aaroh (rise), Avroh (fall) in voice its knowledge depends upon Kak Pathya use. In Vachik Abhinaya six types of Alankars are used and their positions have been described.

Main relationship of Vachik Abhinaya is not with the body but with various experimentation with the voice.

3. **Aharya Abhinaya**—In the four categories of Abhinaya, Aharya has third place. Acharya Nandikeshwar has mentioned that the Natya (drama) which is performed after being adorned with garlands (Haar) and Kayur is called Aharya. Thus Aharya Abhinaya is related to cosmetics, costume and ornaments. Acharya Bharat has named it Nepathya (sideline). In this Nepathya Karma,

the performer should fully know about cosmetics and adornments of various body parts from head to toe together with methods of adorning various ang pratyang according to region, time, caste, condition etc. Aharya is representation of character in natural form with costumes and adornments. For example, for enacting the role of Lava and Kush, boys of less than 12 years of age are suitable and the costume, ornaments etc of these boys should not be regal but suited to jungle dwellers like ornaments made of wild flowers. If proper attention is not paid to these aspects then the Abhinaya can not be called Aharya. Dress is such a medium through which one can gain knowledge about any person's nativity, caste, etc. and it is necessary that it is kept natural.

The importance of cosmetics and adornments is not only for Abhinaya but also for pleasure, beauty, good fortune and well being.

In the scriptures relating to poetry four types of Aharya have been described i.e. (1) Pust (2) Alankar (3) Angrachana (4) Sanjeev

- Pust—Three types of pust (stage) is made by using clothes or hide on Bamboo or sticks. These can be depicted through activities.
- In Alankar Aharya, use of ornaments has been considered. In adornments, various types of garlands, ornaments and hair styles have been considered. The Alankars for males and females have been separately enumerated. In this discussion, attention has been paid to regional aspect, time, social condition, circumstances and age.
- The third ang of Aharya Abhinaya is Angrachana or changing of face/shape. In Ang Rachana many types of dress code for males and females have been described.
- Fourth type of Aharya Abhinaya is Sanjeev. In this the entry of animals and display on the stage is called Sanjeev and for this purpose 'Masks' are used.

In this way Aharya has an important place in Natya and despite being a part of Abhinaya its purpose was Nepathya Rachana i.e. on the sidelines.

In Aharya Abhinaya many traditional Natya and folk styles are used. The purpose of Aharya Abhinaya is to display the living style and culture of the world. In Aharya Abhinaya the character appears on the stage putting on the role of original character. He adopts the form of original character to the extent possible, in so far as its nature, state of mind, region, caste, etc and comes on the stage and by using his voice and Aangik activities provides a dynamic display of life flow of this world.

4. Satvik Abhinaya—In the various categories of Abhinaya, Satvik Ahinaya has fourth and last place and its importance is self evident. Acharya Bharat while establishing its supremacy has mentioned that the Natya (drama) in which Satvik Abhinaya is prominent, is considered of highest order and where its prominence is equal to that of other types of Abhinaya, the natya is considered of medium order. However, the natya in which Satvik Abhinaya is not prominent or absent is called inferior (Adham)

Acharya Abhinav Gupta in his Abhinav Bharti has mentioned that the Abhinaya is actually Satvik Abhinaya and not Aangik, Vachik or Aharya. It is said that the Nat (performer) acts which means that his state of mind has harmonised with the state of mind of character *i.e.* Rama, Nayakas.

From this angle Natya is considered to be based on satva (reality). In Abhinaya Darpan while describing the characteristics of Satvik Abhinaya, it is mentioned that the natya in which Bhavagya (one who understands Bhavas) performs a dance through the medium of Satvik Bhavas, is called Satvik Abhinaya.

Eight types of Satvik Bhavas have been described (1) Stambhan (statue like) (2) Sweating profusely (3) extreme surprise (4) stammering of voice (5) tremors in body (6) distortion of face (7) weeping (8) fainting. It is stated in Natya Shastra that sadness, fainting, shame, hatred, grief, guilt feeling, dreaming, slumber, anxiety, restriction etc. Bhavas and their various stages should be exhibited through Satvik Bhavas.

Thus among various categories of Abhinaya, the greatness of Satvik Abhinaya is self evident. The manner in which the feeling of Satva arises in the mind of appreciating audience can be understood only with the knowledge of Satvik Bhavas.

It is stated in Natya Shastra that 'Satva' originates only with the concentration of mind. The feeling of extreme surprise or tearfall or turning pale of face are the nature of 'Satva'. To enact them and use them, concentration of mind is essential. In Natya the enactment of Lokswabhava (worldly nature) and Lokcharit (worldly character) is through satva. For example in Natya the feeling of pleasure as well as sadness which are worldly feelings are enacted and for expressing these feelings, Satvik Bhavas should be used in a realistic manner.

7. THE TEN PRANS OF TAAL

The origin of word Taal is likely from Tandava and Lasya. Taal is used in singing, instrument playing and dancing. Taal emanates from 'Chhand' *i.e.* 'Chhand Laya' formed by various Matras gives rise to Taals. In common parlance the meter for 'Laya' is called Tall.

In composing the 'Taal' following ten components are considered important.

Kalo Margi Kriyangani Gruho Jati Kala-Layah
Yati Prastar Kashyati Taal Pranah Dashsmritah

Kaal, Marg, Kriya, Gruh, Jati, Laya, Yati and Prastar are the ten characterstics of Taal.

1. **Kaal**—In music, time is called Kaal. To understand Kaal, the Taal is divided into Matra and Vibhag (parts)

2. **Marg**—The movement of Kaal from first Matra to last Matra of any 'Taal' is called Marg.

3. **Kriya**—The action of demonstrating Taal on the palm is called Kriya. Kriya is of two types. When we clap it is called 'Sashabd Kriya' (Kriya with sound) and when Matras are counted either by moving fingers or any other body part but without clapping it is called 'Nihshabd Kriya' (soundless Kriya). These two types of Kriya also has many sub types.

Types of 'Sashabd Kriya'—

(i) *Dhrava*—To move the hands down while making sounds by striking thumb against middle finger.
(ii) *Shampa*—To strike on left hand by right hand.
(iii) *Taal*—To strike on right hand by left hand.
(iv) *Sannipaat*—To strike mutually with both hands.

Types of Nihshabd Kriya—

(i) *Avaap*—To contract the fingers while raising the hands upward.

(ii) *Nishkaam*—To bring down the palm and extend the fingers.

(iii) *Vikshep*—To move the open left hand to the right so that the face of palm is held vertically up.

(iv) *Pravesh*—To contract the finger while holding the hand downwards.

4. **Anga**—To count the Kaal in Taal, the meter used is called Anga. A total of eight Angas are described in the scriptures.

Number	*Name*	*Matra*	*Sign*
1	Anuvrat	¼	∪
2	Drat	½	O
3	Dratviram	¾	∪̥
4	Laghu	1	|
5	Laghuviram	1¼	Y
6	Guru	2	S
7	Plut	3	S
8	Kakpad	4	+

5. **Gruh**—The Matra of Taal from which the song commences is called Gruh or 'Samgruh' of any Taal. Gruh are of four types.

(a) *Sama Gruh*—When the song or Tukda begins or concludes after the 'sama' of Taal, then it is called Samgruh.

(b) *Visham Gruh*—When the song or Tukda does not begin from first Matra of any Taal but from any other Matra, it is called Visham Gruh.

(c) *Anaghaat*—When the singer or dancer hides the 'sam' of 'Taal' in such a manner that the song or Tukda would appear to end before sam it is called 'Anaghaat'.

(d) *Ateet Gruh*—When the singer or dancer hides in 'sam' and ends the Taal or Tukda in such a manner that it appears that the Tukda is coming after Sam, it is called 'Ateet Gruh'

6. **Jati**—Jati denotes the 'Laghu Matras' in any 'Taal', It has an important place in the construction of 'Taal'. In any Taal, change of Laghu Matras according to Jati results in composition of a new Taal. Jatis are of five types:

(i) *Tistra Jati*—The Jati constructed by three Matras is called Tistra Jati.

(ii) *Chatustra*—The Jati constituted by four matras is called Chatustra.

(iii) *Khanda Jati*—On account of division of Jati, it is called Khanda Jati.

$$(4/2 + 3) = (2 + 3) = 5$$

(iv) *Mistra Jati*—Mistra Jati originates from a combination of Tistra and Chatustra Jati.

$$(3 + 4) = 7$$

(v) *Sankeerna*—Mixing of Chatustra Jati in Khanda Jati gives rise to Sankeerna Jati.

$$(4/2 + 3) + 4 = 9$$

7. **Kala**—The art or style of playing Tabla or Pakhawaj is called Kala. In each Gharana, there is a peculiar style of 'Nikasi' of Bols and therefore Gharanas are formed on the basis of Kala.

8. **Laya**—The speed of time is called Laya. Laya are of three types viz. Vilambit, Madhya and Drut.

9. **Yati**—The nature of Laya is called Yati. Various Layakaris are born from the Yati. Five types of Yatis are described in the scriptures.

(i) *Samayati*—Uniform speed of Laya is called Samayati.

(ii) *Strotgatayati*—The manner in which the speed of waterfall is first Vilambit and then Madhya and finally Drut is called Strotgatayati.

(iii) *Gopuchhayati*—Just like the tail of cow is first broad and then becomes thin, the Laya in Gopuchhayati, first becomes Drut and then Vilambit. This is called 'Gopuchhayati'

(iv) *Mrudangayati*—The two ends of Mrudung are small and the middle part is large. Like Mrudang the Laya is Drut in the beginning and at the end and is Vilambit in middle in Mrudangayati. It has three sub types *i.e.*

(a) Vilambit at the beginning and in the end and Drut in the middle

(b) Madhya at the beginning and in the end Drut in the middle and

(c) Vilambit in the beginning and the end and Madhya in the middle.

(v) *Pipilikayati*—Yati like an ant or Damroo which is just opposite of Mrudangayati is called Pipilikayati. It has three sub types.

(i) Drut in the beginning and end and Vilambit in middle.

(ii) Drut in the beginning and end and Madhya in middle.

(iii) Madhya in the beginning and middle and Vilambit in middle.

10. **Prastaar**—It implies extending any Taal through Kayada, Patta, Reta, Tukda etc.

8. STANDARD WORDS RELATING TO DANCE

1. **Anulome**—To come forward in a diagonal manner
2. **Andaj**—It means style or manner. When the dancer presents a 'Tukda' 'Bol' or emotes through peculiar action(s) then it is called 'andaj'.
3. **Anubhav**—The expressions which enable understanding of Vachikam, Aangikam and Satvik abhinaya are called 'Anubhav'. In dance and drama, emotions are identified with these expressions and Mudras.
4. **Abhinaya**—When the dancer in the course of dance acts out someone else's actions, it is called' Abhinaya' e.g. Acting out the emotions/actions of Yashoda in feeding curd to Krishna in 'Makhan Leela'. In 'Natyashastra' of Bharat four types of acting are 'described:
   (a) *Angik*—through limbs
   (b) *Vachik*—through speech
   (c) *Aharya*—through dress or costume
   (d) *Satvik*—through expressions
5. **Anga**—Various parts of human body are called' Anga'. In dance mainly 6 parts of human body are considered *i.e.* head, hand, chest, sides, waist and feet.
6. **Anghar**—Main mudras based on minute Mudras (Karans) are called 'Anghar', 'Anghars' are created through combination of seven, eight or nine Karans. In Bharat's Natyashastra, a total of thirty two 'Anghars' are described.
7. **Ada**—When during emoting *i.e.* depicting an emotion or dancing, the dancer performs in a stylish manner, it is called 'Ada'.
8. **Anchit**—In the course of dance, when the dancer hits the ground with heels while lifting the frontal portion of feet, it is called' Anchit'.

9. **Arthabhav**—When the dancer performs on a poem and becomes a role player in the subject of the poem, it is called' Arthabhav'.
10. **Anukaran Mudra**—When during the course of performance, the dancer depicts any subject with the help of hands and limbs (Anga) of the body, it is called 'Anukaran Mudra'.
11. **Agratal**—Striking the ground with the frontal portion of the feet is called 'Agratal'.
12. **Amad**—Amad means 'entry'. When the dancer performs a Tukda while entering the stage, it is called Tukda of Amad.
13. **Aalidh**—To sit by kneeling is called Alidh.
14. **Avartan**—The duration from Sama to Sama in any Taal is called Avartan.
15. **Aadh**—When one and half matra is taken in the duration of one matra or six matras are taken in the duration of four matras, then that laya is called Aadh.
16. **Akashchari**—When in the course of dance, the dancer performs with one leg then it is called' Akashchari. In Natyashastra Akashcharis of following six team types have been described.

    Atikranta, Apkranta, Parshvakranta, Urdhvajanu, Suchi, Nupurpadika, Dolapad, Akshipta, Aviddha, Udvruta, Vidhudrabhranta, Alata, Bhujangtrasita, Mrugpluta, Danda, Bhramari.
17. **Ishtpad**—When during the course of dance performance, the dancer prays to lord by exhibiting the Bhavas of Kavitt and Ishtparanas, then it is called Ishtpad.
18. **Urap**—The way Garud or an Eagle leaps in the process of flying in the same way the dancer leaps in the air gladly to express the state of excitement which is called Urap.
19. **Urmai**—When the dancer leaps in the air in a manner which shows as if he is hung in the middle i.e. he touches the ground sometime after taking the leap, it is called Urmai. For example in the Raas, Radha performs Urmai by putting her arms around

the neck of Krishna and then puts her head on the shoulder of Krishna after taking a circular motion in the air.

20. **Uthan**—After prayer, the first Tukda of dance is called Uthan. Uthan is the first Bol of dance which establishes Kathak dance.
21. **Kasak**—The movement of wrist in the dance according to Taal is called Kasak or Kalas.
22. **Kataksh**—To look with an askewed glance is called Kataksh. In Drishti Bhed it is considered similar to Sachi Drishti. The dancers generally use it in Thath, Sama or while emoting.
23. **Kuadi**—When five matras are taken in the duration of four matras then that Laya is called Savaiyya or Kuadi.
24. **Karan**—Combined movement of hand and feet in the dance is called Karan. In Bharat Natyashastra 108 types of Karan are described.
25. **Kunchit**—In the dance performance when the heel is lifted and the ground is struck with the front portion of foot and then the foot is taken behind the other foot, it is called Kunchit.
26. **Kala**—Two Matras form one Kala. Tal division is called Kala.
27. **Kunchit Bhramari**—The circular motion while contracting the knees is called Kunchit Bhramari.
28. **Kuttan**—Striking of ground with feet is called Kuttan.
29. **Kriya**—The process of doing is called Kriya.
30. **Kavitta**—Any poem or pada is called Kavitt. In the dance along with Kavitta its Bhav is also exhibited.
31. **Khali**—After Sama at the time of showing division, when the hand is moved to one side in the air it is called Khali or Phank.
32. **Greeva Sanchalan**—The movement of neck in the dance is called Greeva Sanchalan. Abhinaya Darpan describes four types of Greeva Sanchalan.
    (a) *Sundari Greeva*—movement to left and right.
    (b) *Tirschina Greeva*—the neck which is moved sideways like that of serpent.
    (c) *Parivartita Greeva*—movement of neck in a half moon shaped manner.

(d) *Prakampita Greeva*—Backward forward movement of neck like that of a pigeon.

33. **Gatbhava**—During the course of dance, when the dancer takes up a short storyline and exhibits the same along with Laya it is called Gatbhava.
34. **Gat Nikas**—While dancing, the dancer takes a particular Hastak and moves in a Bhavpurna manner. This movement according to Laya is called Gat Nikas.
35. **Gati Bhava**—It is narration of a story which can be composed in a Thumari.
36. **Gatibhed**—In the course of dance, when the movement shows the movements of various animals, birds etc. by using a particular Hastak or Bhava, it is called Gatibhed. In Abhinaya Darpan 10 types movements have been described such as Hansi Gati, Mayurigati, Mrugigati, Gajleela, Turanginigati, Singhi Gati, Mandukigati, Veeragati, Manavigati, Bhujangigati.
37. **Gat Arth Bhava**—In the course of dance when the dancer himself sings and explains the Bhava and then dances it is called Gat Arth Bhava.
38. **Gat**—It has no Tukda or Tihai but through Gat a specific Bhav is expressed in the dance. In percussion instruments a composition of soft Bols is called Gat.
39. **Guru**—A teacher in any specific sphere is called revered Guru.
40. **Gat Palta**—Before commencing Gatnikas when right hand is moved over the head and a round is taken and when this procedure is repeated from the left side it is called Gat Palta.
41. **Ghunghat**—While dancing when the dancer expresses the bhava of Ghunghat then this action is called Ghunghat.
42. **Ghumariya**—A circular motion or Bhramari while dancing is called Ghumariya. In Abhinaya Darpan seven types of Ghumariyas have been mentioned *i.e.* Utplut Bhramari, Chakrabhramari, Garadbhramari, Ekpad Bhramari, Kunchit Bhramari, Akash Bhramari, Ang Bhramari.
43. **Chari**—The process of lifting one foot and then putting it down in the dance is called Chari. In Abhinaya Darpan eight types

of charis are described i.e. Chalan Chari, Chakramanchari, Saranchari, Veginichari, Kuttanchari, lulitchari, lolitchari, Vishamchar chari.

44. **Chakkardar Toda**—When the dancer repeats any bol three times and arrives at Sam then it is called Chakkardar Toda.
45. **Chougun**—When four matras are taken in the duration of one matra, it is called Chougun.
46. **Chakkardar Paran**—When in the dance 'Tiyedar' bol of Pakhawaj are repeated three times it is called Chakkardar Paran.
47. **Chalan**—The process of moving from one place to another is called Chalan.
48. **Jamanka**—The dancer when sits on stage with ghunghat the posture is called Jamanka.
49. **Jatishunya**—In this 'Bhava' and 'Ang' are exhibited through the medium of 'Laya'.
50. **Jatiparan**—In the dance that group of bols of Pakhawaj or Tukda which is based on a particular Jati is called Jatiparan.
51. **Jati**—In the division of Taal when the number of Matras change then the Jati of Taal changes. Jatis are of five types i.e. Tistra, Chutastra, Khand, Mishra and Sankeerna.
52. **Thath**—In the beginning of dance when the dancer stands in a special pose and uses Kasak, Masak and Kalas in a Laya then it is called 'Thath'. No Bhavas are demonstrated in Thath; only movement of various ang, upang and pratyang is made in a beautiful manner.
53. **Theka**—The definite bol of any Taal is called 'Theka'. Theka is played either on Tabla or Pakhawaj.
54. **Thah**—When one matra is taken in the deviation of one matra, it is called Thah Laya.
55. **Thumri**—It is a musical composition of Northern India in which nature of Nayika or her condition is described. Thumri compositions are often chiefly Shringarik on the basis of which dancers demonstrate Bhavas through Abhinaya.

56. **Tatkar**—In the course of dance the sounds which are produced by striking feet on the ground are called Tatkar i.e. Ta, Thai, Tat Taa, Thai, Thai, Tat.
57. **Toda**—The group of Talbaddha Bols in the dance is called Toda which comprises various Layas and Tihai.
58. **Taal**—A group of definite Matras is called Taal.
59. **Tirap**—Slanted movement in dance is called Tirap.
60. **Taiyyari**—When the dancer practices difficult bols, footwork or Tukdas to such an extent that he/she could perform them in Drut (fast) Laya easily, it is called Taiyyari. Taiyyari includes neatness and swiftness in performance of Tatkar, body movements and Bhava demonstration.
61. **Taali**—After Sama at the time of exhibiting division when a clap is given then, it is called Taali or Bhari.
62. **Tihai**—When in a dance a group of bols are repeated thrice before arriving at Sama it is called Tihai viz.

    Ta the E ta Thai Ta the E ta Thai Ta the E ta
63. **Totak Da Trotak**—Trotak is the first in the table of twenty Nritya bhedas. This is 'Varna Vrutt' whose each charan has four Sangan
64. **Tipalli**—When any Bol is sequentially repeated in Thath, Dun, Chougun, Layas it is called Tipalli. ,—
65. **Tharr**—When the tip of big toe of the feet is grounded and rubbed the sound produced is called Tharr.
66. **Drut Laya**—Very swift Laya is called Drut Laya.
67. **Damdar**—In the course of dance when at the end of a Palla in a Tihai or Chhakardar Tukda the dancer particularly halts it is called Damdar Tukda or Tihai
68. **Dugun**—When two matras are taken in the duration of one matra it is called Dugun.
69. **Dhilang**—That part in which the dancer leaps up in enjoyment and then lands on the ground is called Dhilang.
70. **Navhakka**—When in the last Tihai of a paran continuously Nine Dha are used, it is called Navhakka.

71. **Nrityang**—In this, various forms of dance are demonstrated in which together with repetition (Avrithi) of taals, Layakari Jati and pronunciation of Talkars are included.
72. **Naaj**—Naaj means Nakhra—In this the dancer performs proudly with pomp and show.
73. **Nikas**—Movement from one Mudra to another in the course of dance is called Nikas. The dancer emotively moves the body parts, strikes the ground in any Matra of the Taal and moves from one place to another, adopts an attractive posture and stands. Some learned persons call the process of returning after conclusion of dance as Nikas.
74. **Pathant**—In the course of dance to explain the peculiarity of a Tukda, the dancer reads out the bols of Tukda on Taal before the audience and this process is called Pathant.
75. **Paran**—The group of powerful bols of dance which has 2, 3, 4 or more Avruttis (repetition) is called paran.
76. **Palta**—Changing of sequence of bols in various ways in dance, singing and instrument playing is called Palta.
77. **Pad Vinyas**—The process of taking a step in the dance is called Pad Vinyas.
78. **Pratilom**—The process of moving backwards is called Pratilom or Vilom.
79. **Puhuppunjari**—In the course of dance performance when the dancer demonstrates the offering of flowers to the God, it is called Puhuppunjari.
80. **Primlu**—This is a distorted form of the word Parimal. When the dancer performs by mixing the bols, and bols of Pakhawaj etc., it is called Primlu.
81. **Pakshiparan**—When in the bols of dance, the bols of various birds are included while dancing then it is called Nrityabol Pakshiparan.
82. **Pindi**—Various changes in the dance are called Pindi. Various dances have different Pindis. There are twelve Pindis in Kathak and eight in Bharat Natyam.

83. **Pindbandh**—Pindbandh is a peculiar shape of dance in which Anghar and Karans are preplanned.
84. **Pratyang**—Those parts of body which can be easily turned are called Pratyang. There are six in dance i.e. Neck, shoulder, back, arms, thighs and hips.
85. **Phiran**—When the dancer proceeds forward while exhibiting a move and then returns back in the same mudra in the Dugun Laya, then the process of returning back is called phiran.
86. **Farmaishi chakkardar**—When any group of bols with Tihai are presented three times, then it is called Farmaishi Chakkardar.
87. **Bol Paran**—When in the dance, literary piece is also included along with bols of Pakhawaj it is called Bolparan.
88. **Bedum**—When at the end of palla of any chakkardar Tukda or Tihai another palla is started immediately without a pause then it is called Bedum Tukda or Tihai.
89. **Bolbhava**—In the course of performance of a song or Thumri, the explanation of meaning of its bols is called Bolbhava
90. **Bhangibhed**—Bhangibhed or Bhangimabhed are synonymous words. Bhangi means slant or wickedness. When the dancer in a posture stands with his body slanted at one or two or three places then this mudra is called Ekbhang, Dwibhang or Tribhang respectively.
91. **Bhava**—'Bhavayanatititi Bhava' *i.e.* those who create feeling are called Bhava, Without Bhava the dance is meaningless. In Kathak dance seven ways of expressing Bhavas are common. These are Nayan Bhava, Bolbhava. Arthbhava, Sabhabhava, Nrityabhava, Gatarthbhava and Angbhava.
92. **Bhavrang**—In this Nayak—Nayika Bheds are expressed on the basis of Sahityaparan, Bhav paran and Swar Jati.
93. **Bhumichari**—When both feet are grounded it is called Bhumichari. In Natyashastra sixteen types of Bhumicharis are described—sampada, sthitavarta, shakatasya, adhyardhika, chakshgati, vichyava, edkakridita, baddha, urudvruta, adidta, utspandita, janita, syandita, apsyandita, samotsarifamattalli, mattalli.

94. **Bhavmudra**—Bhavmudra reflects the feelings of the heart. Various internal feelings are reflected in eyes, on brows, face etc., and its reaction can be seen on other parts of the body which is called Bhavmudra.
95. **Bhramari**—When the dancer takes rounds continuously while standing at one place it is called Bhramari or Chakra.
96. **Madhyalaya**—The laya which is neither very slow nor very fast is called Madhyalaya.
97. **Masak**—In Masak the shoulders are moved in a circular fashion in which chest and lower sides are also helpful. In this process, the female dancer moves the breasts by inhaling/exhaling.
98. **Matra**—The measurement of time in music is called Matra. Matra is bigger in Vilambitlaya, ordinary in Madhya Laya and short in Drutlaya.
99. **Mudra**—various shapes formed by using hands, in the course of dance are called Mudras. These are of two types (i) non-composite (Asanyukta) Mudra and (ii) Composite (Sanyukta) Mudra.
100. **Mandal**—A group of three or four parts is called a Mandai. In abhinaya Darpan a total of ten Mandals have been described i.e. Sthanak, Aayat, Alidh, Pratyalidh, Prekhan, Prerit, Swastik, Motit, Samasuchi, Parshwasuchi.
101. **Malkriya**—The process of moving hands in various directions is called Malkriya. It is of seven types :
    (a) *Vishnumal*—because there is only one Vishnu
    (b) *Jeevmal*—Jeev (life) is of two numbers, Jeevatma (Soul) Parmatma (God)
    (c) Gunmal—Gun (quality) are three; Sata, Raja and Tama
    (d) *Yugmal*—Yug (ages) are four; Satyug, Tretayug, Dwapar and Kaliyug.
    (e) *Tatvamal*—Tatva (elements) are five; Jal (water) Tej (fire), Vayu (air), Prithvi (earth) and Akash (sky)
    (f) *Ritumal*—Ritu (seasons) are six; Vasant (spring), Greeshma (summer), Varsha (rains), Sharad (winter), Hemant (autumn), shishir (extreme cold)

(g) *Lokmal*—Loks (worlds) are seven; Bhuh, Bhuvah, Swah, Mahh, Janah, Tapah and Satya Lok.

102. **Mukhvilas**—In the course of dance, the shy and hesitant expression of pleasure on the face of dancer is called Mukhvilas.

103. **Mukhda**—After commencement of theka on a percussion instrument when a small bol is played, it is called Mukhda.

104. **Rechaka**—The Layabaddha movement of body parts is called Rechaka. It is mainly of four types *i.e.* Pad Rechak, Kati Rechak, Hast Rechak, and Greeva Rechak.

105. **Rang**—On the stage the Nata and Nati feel happy through entertaining each other.

106. **Laagdat**—In this process the dancer, for the entertainment of audiences, uses various tricks to arrive at Sama. This is also called Jugalbandi, for example the tabla player plays any chhand on Sama and leaves at the 8th Matra and the dancer cleverly picks up from 9th Matra and leaves at the 16th Matra. This means that one of them applies dat while the other in reply tells Laag.

107. **Laya**—In music the speed of singing, instrument playing or dancing is called Laya. It is of three types i.e. Vilambit, Madhya and Drut.

108. **Vyuh Kriya**—In the course of group dances, when the dancers together form different shapes, it is called Vyuh Kriya i.e. Trikona (Triangle), Bana (Arrow), Serpent, Crescent, Well, Octagon, Quadrilateral, Sopan (Stairs), Rana (fight) and Pataka (flag)

109. **Vilambit Laya**—Very slow Laya is called Vilambit Laya

110. **Vibhav**—Vibhav means reason or purpose i.e. on account of kidnapping of Sita, Rama felt anger towards Ravana. It is of two types :

(a) *Alamban*—upon seeing which a sthyaee bhava (permanent feeling) is generated.

(b) *Uddipan*—the means of awakening a Bhava (feeling) is called Uddipan.

111. **Vibhag**—Each Taal has some natural parts which are called Vibhag. For example there are four Vibhag (parts) in Teen Taal Jhap Taal.
112. **Viadi**—When seven Matras are taken in the duration of four Matras then it is called one and three quarter Gun (Paune dogun) or Viadi Laya.
113. **Baant**—the process of dividing into various parts and Layas by taking a Laggi and making Paltes out of it.
114. **Shobha**—the appearance of Shringarik glow on the body parts of Nayika is called Shobha.
115. **Stuti**—The hymn or Shloka rendered in the prayer of God, Goddess or teacher in the beginning of the dance is called Stuti.
116. **Salami**—This word is derived from Muslim style. When a dancer after performing any Toda or Tukda shows salutation to the audience on Sama it is called Salami.
117. **Sarpayan**—Movement like a serpent in the dance is called Sarpayan.
118. **Sulap**—It means flexible and delicate. Just like the flame of a lamp flickers in the air, the dancer delicately moves his body in same manner which is called Sulap. In Sulap, Lasya is main ang.
119. **Sam**—The first Matra of each Taal is called Sam. On Sam, first clap is done and a peculiar stress is laid.
120. **Samput**—To contract any bloomed object is called Samput.
121. **Hastak**—The movement of hands in the course of dance is called Hastak. Some learned persons call it Malkriya also.
122. **Tribhang**—It is the name of a special posture of Lord Krishna in which Krishna is shown to stand while slanting knee, waist and neck (with three turns in the body, the posture is called Tribhang).

9. ACCESSORIES USED IN KATHAK DANCE

For a successful dance performance, proficiency in art is definitely required apart from intelligent use of dancing accessories. These accessories are (i) Stage arrangement (ii) Light and sound system (iii) Make up (iv) Costume and (v) Background music.

1. **Stage arrangement**—In ancient times dance performances were held in temples. There was no provision for stage. The dancer used to perform in the temple courtyard in front of Gods. Later on when dances were patronized by the courts of kings even then stage was not required.

It was at a much later date when art of dance came out of temples and courts, for the entertainment of public, it became necessary to have a stage. Today importance of stage in dance performance has increased manifold. Before dance performance, the dancer pays attention to the place of performance. Theatres are not available at all places and usually at such places temporary stages are constructed by joining wooden planks but if proper care is not taken then planks may not be kept at level or space is left in the joints, making it difficult to dance. The dancer may have his/her feet caught in the cleft between planks and hurt his/her feet. Sometimes the planks are covered by carpets but it makes demonstration of footwork by the dancer difficult. In fact, for Kathak dance, stage made of cement or stone is required. Kathak dance particularly involves intricate footwork which requires cement or stone flooring for proper performance. The stage should be at least 18' x 15' and 3' above the ground level. Stage should also have curtains, side wings, light and adequate place for singer and instrument players.

2. **Light and Sound arrangement**—Today, light and sound have become a must without which no performance can be possible. In older times singers and actors used to have loud voice which could be heard clearly even from substantial distance without the

help of any equipment and the instruments used in the performance were also loud with echo effect. After invention of sound equipments, the singers do not need to exercise their vocal chords to the same degree. Even whispering voice of the actors can now be heard clearly by the audience.

Today, sound equipments and sound effects are used effectively and the Tape recorder has proved to be very useful in this matter. The thunder of clouds, noise of rain and lightening, tempest, voices of animals and birds are pre-recorded on tape and then played in the course of performance when needed. This process is called sound composition.

This being scientific age, electric light has turned out to be a boon for dance performance. In olden times dance performance, in the absence of light arrangement, usually took place in the day light and only at times in the night by using large lamps and fire torches. Modern days stage performance is known for minute light arrangement so essential for dance/drama enactment.

The dance stages have special light arrangement. Electrical bulbs are fixed on the floor, roof and on the sides which glow with varied intensity at different times and enhance the quality of dance performance. With the help of electrical equipments, scenes can be depicted in a moment and in rapid succession.

Primarily, stage light arrangement can be divided into 4 categories—

(a) Foot light and Top light
(b) Intense light
(c) Spot light
(d) Lanterns fitted with lenses

Modern light arrangement involves use of dimmer also, enabling variation in the intensity of light.

3. **Make up**—Make up was extremely important even in ancient times. This is proved by the fact that the tribals have the practice of colouring and decorating various parts of their bodies. Initially, this practice was followed, perhaps, to demonstrate the identity of their respective tribe and to attract the companion. With

the development of civilisation and simultaneous development of artistic aspect of dance and emergence of its classical form, the rules of make up were laid down and separate books were written on this subject.

As mentioned in 'Sangeet Ratnakar' regarding make up, at the outset one should cleanse the body by using 'ubtan' and then take bath with water which energises the body. After this cream should be applied to the face and daubed with light pink powder. Kajal should be applied to the eyes and lipstick to the lips. Eyebrows should be given shape by using an eyebrow pencil. Rouge should be touched upon the cheeks. 'Mehandi' should be applied to the hands and 'Alta' to the feet. 'Bindi' or 'Tilak' should be applied on the forehead. Hairstyle should be according to the role. Kundal, Bale (Ear rings), Amulet, Waist band, Kavach, Manibandh, anklets are the ornaments commonly put on by the performer.

Make up in modern times—Attention should be paid to the following aspect in modern make up. The face should be washed with hot water and immediately thereafter with cold water. Soap can also be used to wash the face which provides shine and vitality to the skin. Some performers use cleansing milk and astringent prior to make up to remove the dirt from the skin. If the dancer has black shadows under the skin she can fill it with light coloured panstick. After it dries out, foundation or pancake should be uniformly applied to entire face by using a sponge. Thereafter, nose, chin, cheeks should be applied with a little more colour to make them prominent. Eyebrows should be raised and their outline should be made pronounced by light use of 'Kajal pencil' and Kajal should be applied to the eyes. From the eyes to the temples, a line should be drawn by using Kajal in a manner to suit the face.

Some dancers use eye shadow. Eye shadow should be selected to match with the colour of costume. The colour of lipstick should also match with the colour of costume. Black pencil should be used to make faint outline.

This completes the make up of the dancers.

4. **Costume**—Any dance can be identified with the costume worn by the dancer. Costume adds a peculiar charm to the dance. From ancient times costumes have been undergoing change. The costume for Kathak dance is simple. In Jaipur Gharana, the dancers wear churidar pyjama, sherwani, Jaridar cap and tie a dupatta from neck to waist. The dancers from Lucknow Gharana wear churidar pyjama, kalidar kurta and embellished jacket. The same dress is worn by female dancers also. The costumes have, however, changed. Today male dancers wear 'Langdar Dhoti' with a waist band. Upper part of the body is bare. They wear Bajuband in hand, Kundal in ears and necklace in neck. Female dancers wear Ghaghara with flares and blouse with a Dupatta.

5. **Background Music**—Today, background music is an important part of any theatre performance. Bharat Muni in the five chapters of his Natyashastra, has described in great detail, Swar, Shruti, Murchana, Jati, Atidhi Vidhan and Giti and their various variations and how according to Rasa and Bhava, singing and instrument playing should be organised in various parts of drama. Considering this importance of music in drama, Bharat has called it the bed or foundation of drama (Natya).

In the drama experiment of Bharat, Kutup the group of singers and instrument players are seated behind the stage and on the sides in the middle of both entry points and after their being seated, the drama was started with a prayer being offered to the Kutup.

In the Indian tradition, synthesis of all the three *i.e.* singing, instrument playing and dance is called music. Each motion of dance is according to 'Laya' and 'Tal' *i.e.* the dance steps follow the instrument. The theka of 'Tal' follows the tune of the song *i.e.* follows the instrument music.

Today, in order to make dance performance more effective the number of instruments are often increased. Well organised collective instrument playing is actually required to provide background music for bailes (Nritya Natikas).

The composition of background music is a highly skilled, technical work and requires a great deal of imagination on the part of composer.

6. **Kutup**—Kutup means collective instrument playing (Vrind-Vadan) *i.e.* many instruments are played together in tune with each other. Kutup was used in ancient times also. According to certain learned persons, Kutup finds a mention in old scriptures also.

To construct or compose, Kutup requires an able music director since many artists work under him. It is a difficult job. First of all the instruments are identified and then the artists to play them. The music director uses some artists in the entire Kutup and some in special pieces.

For Kutup each artist rehearses separately and then all artists rehearse together. Thus with a few days' efforts Kutup comes to final shape.

In modern days, Kutup is quite popular in classical music and dance. Use of Kutup has enlivened the -Abhinaya & Bhavas' of dance. Movement of limbs according to tals following the tunes of various instruments brings beauty to the dance.

Kutup is a necessary accessory for Bailes which are very popular these days. In Bailes to depict thunder of clouds, tempest, rains, etc., and various Rasas Kutup has made significant contribution.

●●●

4

1. NATYA, NRIT AND NRITYA

Before the development of language, human beings used to exchange their thoughts through movement of body parts and emoting. The development of civilisation and the artistic acting, gave birth to Natya and the 'Laya' in the heart of humans combined to result in the development of dance (Nritya).

Natya : Acting according to a story is called Natya. This is also called Rupak. In Natya following four types of acting are used : (a) Angik; (b) Vachik; (c) Aharya and (d) Satvik.

Nrit : Movement of body parts according to Tal but without Bhava is called Nrit. Some learned persons call body movement or foot work according to Tal as Nrit.

Nritya : Rasabhavavyan janadi Yukt, the performance which has Rasa Bhav and Vyanjana *i.e.* expression is called Nritya *i.e.* dance, It has beautiful combination of Bhava and Laya.

2. SELECTION AND USE OF ANKLETS (GHUNGHROOS)

In every Indian dance Ghunghroos (anklets) are used. According to Abhinaya Darpan anklets should be made of bronze but these days anklets of brass are common which are tied on a blue tape rope at small distances of say 3/4" to 1", total number of bells being hundred to two hundred on one feet.

For successful performance, the dancer should have total command over anklets which requires daily practice (riyaz). The anklets should be tied very tightly from ankles upwards. The anklets should not get loosened while dancing but should not be so tight so as to cut into the skin of legs.

Before use of anklets, a cotton tape can be wound on the legs which would prevent the rope of anklets from cutting into the skin. This practice is commonly used by all the dancers.

3. GOOD AND BAD QUALITIES OF DANCERS

Dance is a visual art and in its performance one can enjoy simultaneously visual, audio, rasa and emotions.

In the dance performance the dancer should have good built and attractive personality so as to appear pleasant to the eyes of audience.

In 'Abhinaya Darpan' there is vivid description of the qualities of the performer. In Bharat's Natya shastra also detailed knowledge has been imparted about good and bad qualities of the performer. Since dance is considered to be an art form more suited to women, comparatively there is more discussion on good and bad qualities of female dancer than male one.

In the end every participant in the dance has to mould oneself in such a manner so as to provide enough entertainment and pleasure to the audience.

Qualities of female dancer

Female dancer should be beautiful, have attractive limbs and pleasant to the eyes through the medium of art of dancing. The dancer should be accomplished in Taal, have wide eyes and be adept in singing and instrument playing. She should have total command on her art before entering the stage. She should not be fat nor should be too thin; neither too tall nor short. She should possess sweet smile, good voice and be capable of imagination. She should wear good clothes and only such a dancer earns respect from the lovers of art.

Bad qualities of female dancer: Dancer with swollen eyes or one who is bald, obese, thin, large lips, too tall, short, hunchbacked, has bad voice is considered too incapable.

Qualities of Male dancer

According to 'Sangeet Ratnakar' the person who daily practices Margi Nrit i.e. Karan performed by Lord Shiva, Anghar, Chari and Rechaks is called a dancer (Nartak) He should be from a good family, knowledgeable in the art of dance, having command on senses, good speaker, active, have body like a bow, expert in singing and instrument playing, possess knowledge of Indian dances, should be good teacher, capable of imagining new things, having good eyesight, arms like a stout creeper and a face which does not reflect effect of labour during the course of dance.

Bad qualities of dancer—The dancer, who is not handsome, obese or thin, too tall or singing short, unskilled in dance, singing and instrument playing, has protruding hips, weak arms, shows effects of labour on face in the course of dancing, incapable of imparting training, does not have knowledge of music or dance, is considered to be an incapable one.

4. SUCCESSFUL PERFORMANCE, RULES, SEQUENCE AND PRECAUTIONS

Every art has to be exhibited according to certain set rules, The artist who performs according to rules of the art, would be able to impress the audience. For successful dance performance, it is necessary that the artist and organisers make all out efforts in advance to ensure its success. Every artist, whether senior or junior should understand this ground rule for successful performance.

Before the commencement of performance, the instrument players occupy their appointed place and thereafter either on Sarangi or on Harmonium Lahra is played in 'Vilambit' Laya. Thereafter Tabla or Mrudung players play an 'Uthan'. After this, the dancer enters the stage and pays respect to his or her 'Guru' and instrument players. This is followed by a prayer to God before commencing the performance. The artist also prays to God for purifying the heavenly and natural disturbances.

After offering prayer to the god, the dancer strikes on initial pose and then demonstrates 'Nikas' of various types and dances 'Amad Toda' After 'Amad' the dancer displays 'Thats'. 'Thats' are usually performed in 'Vilambit' Laya. Thereafter, the dancer performs 'Tode' 'Tukde' 'Paran' and 'Chakkardar Paran' and displays complex 'Layakaris' through footwork which impress the audience. It is necessary for the artist to recite, whatever he or she wants to perform, by giving 'taal' by hand and thereafter dance the same.

In the second stage the dancer increases the 'Laya' and demonstrates 'Todes', 'Paran' 'Raas' 'Todes of Primulu' 'Gat Bhava' and 'emoting'. By this time the dancer achieves high level of activity and elasticity in the body.

Towards the end all artists perform in 'Drut Laya' Here the performance covers various types of 'Tatkar' (footwork), 'Palte' 'Ladi' 'Atit' 'Anagat' and Graha. Sometimes there are queries and replies between the dancer and tabla player. It is in 'Drut' Laya that artist demonstrates special work of anklets (Ghunghroos) and amazes the audience by making sound from a single ghungroo out of hundreds.

For successful performance, it is necessary that 'bol' 'Tukda' etc are sequenced in the order of their increasing effectiveness, Further, before presenting any composition it should be ensured that it would be capable of entertaining the audience.

Sometimes, audience do make noise during the course of performance due to which the dancer loses his or her nerves. However, the dancer should not lose his/her poise and work with patience and resolve. For successful performance, the dancer should be capable of altering the sequence of performance to suit the taste of audience and only then the artist will be able to satisfy the audience.

Before commencing the performances, the artist should well inspect the stage, light, sound arrangements, make-up and costume.

According to Muni Bharat, the success of dance performance depends mainly on three factors; these are dancer, experiment and prosperity. Wherever these factors combine, the success of performance will be ensured.

5. TYPES OF HEAD MOVEMENTS (SHIROBHED)

While dancing, the dancer makes different types of movements with the head, According to 'Abhinaya Darpan' there are nine types of head movements.

(i) *Samshir* : The head should not be too high or too low, should be situated in the middle and still. This is called 'Samshir'.

(ii) *Udwahit Shir* : Looking upwards or raised head is 'Udwahit Shir'.

(iii) *Adhomukh Shir* : Downward head is the' Adhomukh Shir'.

(iv) *Alolit Shir* : When head is moved in circles, it is called 'Alolit Shir'.

(v) *Dhut Shir* : When head is moved laterally i.e. left and right, it is called 'Dhut Shir'.

(vi) *Kampit Shir* : The head being moved upward and downward is called 'Kampit Shir'.

(vii) *Paravrutt Shir* : When the face is turned, the head is called 'Paravrutt'.

(viii) *Utkshipt Shir* : When the head is moved in a manner so that the dancer looks laterally (left and right) and upwards, it is called 'Utkshipt Shir'.

(ix) *Partiwahit Shir* : When the head is moved sideways like a fan, it is called 'Pariwahit Shir'.

6. TYPES OF EYE MOVEMENTS (DRUSHTIBHED)

Large eyes, their movements add to the beauty of human beings. For a dancer, effective eye movements are vital for good 'Abhinaya'. An exceptional dancer always stands out with his/her effective eye movements. Eyes express feelings like fear, surprise, pleasure clearly. In 'Abhinaya Darpan' eight types of eye movements are described.

(i)	Alokit Drushti	:	A moving pupil in open eyes is the' Alokit Drushti'
(ii)	Sachi Drushti	:	Viewing with a slanted glance is called 'Sachi Drushti'
(iii)	Pralokit Drushti	:	Looking sideways is called 'Pralokit Drushti'
(iv)	Milit Drushti	:	Half opened eyes are Milit Drushti
(v)	Ullokit Drushti	:	Looking upwards is called Ullokit Drushti
(vi)	Anuvrutt Drushti	:	Looking upwards and then downwards rapidly is called' Anuvrutt Drushti'
(vii)	Avlokit Drushti	:	Looking downwards is Avlokit Drushti
(viii)	Sam Drushti	:	Looking with standstill eyelids like heavenly nymphs is called 'Sam Drushti'

7. MOVEMENTS OF EYEBROWS BHAUHEN, BHAVEN, BHRUKRUTI OR BHRU—SANCHALAN

The Bharat Muni has described seven movements of eye brows

(i) Sahaj : It is the natural state of eyebrows.

(ii) Utkshep : When the eyebrows are raised upwards according to the need, it is called 'Utkshep'.

(iii) Paton : When eyebrows are lowered, it is called 'Paton'.

(iv) Bhrukruti : Sideways movement or raising upwards of eyebrows is called Bhrukruti.

(v) Chatur : The action of spreading or elongating the eyebrows is called Chatur.

(vi) Kunchit : Bending of eyebrows downwards is called Kunchit.

(vii) Rechit : Raising of only one eyebrow upwards is called Rechit.

●●●

5

1. STORYLINES OF KATHAK

Dances of all styles are based on ancient stories. Kathak dance style is also based on various mythological stories, such as, Ahilya Uddhar, Amrut Manthan, Usha Aniruddh, Urvashi, Kalia Daman, Gangavataran (the descent of river Ganges), Govardhan Dharan, Gaj and Grah (the elephant & crocodile), Tripur Vadh (killing of demon Tripur), Draupadi Cheer Haran (Disrobing of Draupadi), Dashavatar (the ten incarnations of Lord Vishnu), Putna Vadh (Killing of Putna), Panghat Leela(the plays of Lord Krishna on the village well), Mareech Vadh (killing of Mareech, the Rakshas), Maha Raas (the Grand dance of Raas), Madan Dahan (the burning of Cupid), Lakshman Shakti, Waman Avtar (the incarnation of Lord as pigmy), Vishwanitra and Menaka, Surdas, Sudama Leela, Sati Anusuiya etc.

1. **Ahilya Uddhar**—Ahilya, the wife of sage Gautama was extremely beautiful. One day, Indra, a god; transformed himself as Gautama and defiled Ahilya. When sage Gautama came to know about it, he cursed Ahilya "You be of stone just now". Ahilya tried to explain the matter to Gautama and then Gautama told her that she would be relieved of the curse when Lord Rama would pass through this route and touched her with his feet and she would be restored to her womanly form. After some time Lord Rama, along with brother Laxman, on the way to Mithila, passed through the hermitage of Gautama, he touched the stone with his feet and consequently Ahilya was restored to human form. After offering her prayers to Lord Rama, she went to the abode of her husband.

•

2. **Amrut Manthan**—Once upon a time, entire heaven lost its prosperity on account of a curse cast on it by sage Durvasa and the gods lost to demons (Daityas). Then the gods accompanied with Brahma went to Lord Narayan and pleased him with their prayers and narrated their woes to him. The Lord asked the gods to seek co-operation of Daitya and stir the sea to obtain elixir. The Gods were happy and began to stir the sea along with the Daityas in the hope of obtaining elixir. For this purpose Mandar Mountain (Mandarachal) was used as stirrer, the serpent Vasuki was used as rope. The Lord himself assumed the form of a large tortoise and on his one lac yojana (one yojana equivalent to three miles) broad back, the mountain of Mandar was set up for stirring the sea.

As a consequence of stirring the sea, a lethal poison came out which was the sin of water. Lord Shiva consumed this poison but did not allow it to go below his throat which turned blue due to the poisonous effect. Since then Lord Shiva is also known as 'Neel Kanth' (blue throat). Subsequently, with the grace of Lord Narayan Varuni (a drink), Airawat elephnat, goddess Laxmi, Kaustubh Mani, Conch, Parijat Kalpavriksha, Kamdhenu cow, Uchhaishrava horse, moon and Rambha the nymph came out from the sea. At the end Vaidya (physician) Dhanvanari came out. He had a heavenly body and held a white pitcher in his hand which was full of elixir of life (Amrut), There was a clamour among the gods and daityas for the elixir. To resolve the matter, Lord Vishnu used his Mohini Maya. He assumed the form of a charming woman. Seeing this beautiful woman, the gods and daityas both diverted their attention to her. Using her bewitching powers, the woman made the gods and daityas stand separately in queue to distribute the elixir. She started distributing the elixir and whenever she went to daityas, she charmed them with her captivating smile and gestures and the daityas forgot to drink the elixir.

At the time when the gods were drinking the elixir, a daitya named Rahu transformed himself into a god and also started to drink the elixir. At that time he was recognised by Sun and moon who shouted that this god was actually a daitya. Then Lord Shri Hari who had the chakra, forcefully severed Rahu's crowned head but Rahu's head remained alive, his having consumed the elixir. His torso which fell on the ground also remained alive and was known as Ketu. Since then Rahu & Ketu nurse enemity towards sun and moon and keep on eclipsing them perodically.

3. **Usha-Aniruddh**—Aniruddh was the grandson of Lord Krishna. He was married to Usha, the daughter of Banasur, the monarch of Shonitpur. Usha once had a view of Aniruddha in her dreams due to the boon she had received from goddess Parvati. This fact was known to Chitralekha who showed Usha, pictures of many princes which included the picture of Aniruddha. Then Usha told Chitralekha it was Aniruddha who was her beloved.

Using her yogic powers, Chitralekha got Aniruddha kidnapped while he was asleep. She got them married and kept them at a secret place for four months. After some time when Banasur came to know of it, he got Aniruddha imprisoned using his magical powers. When Krishna, Balram and Pradumna came to know about the fate of Aniruddha, they went to war with Banasur and defeated him but granted his life at the request of his mother. Banasur, thereafter, happily arranged the marriage of Aniruddha and Usha and allowed them to go from Shonitpur.

4. **Urvashi**—Urvashi was the most beautiful nymph of heaven. Once while dancing in Indra's court, she was attracted towards King Puru and missed her Taal(beat). This angered Indra and he cursed Urvashi that after this day she should live in the Mrityu Lok (the earth).

Urvashi chose Puru as her husband on the Earth on the condition that if she could see Puru naked she would leave him. Further, Puru should always meet her desires otherwise she would be freed of her curse and return to heaven.

For a long time Urvashi and Pururava lived as husband and wife and had nine sons. With the passage of time the absence of Urvashi was keenly felt in the heaven. The Gandharvas, to create a condition for ending the curse, sent Vishwasu, a Gandharva, to steal Urvashi's sheep. Pururava at that moment was nude and he ran in the same condition, at Urvashi's request to nab Vishwasu.

Taking advantage of the situation the Gandharvas created light and Urvashi saw Puru in nude condition. As a result, Urvashi was freed of her curse and went to heaven.

5. **Kaliya Daman**—Among the various plays of Lord Krishna, Kaliya Daman is a famous deed performed by him. In his childhood, Lord Krishna used to play with ball at Kalideh on the bank of river Yamuna along with his Gwala (cowherd) friends.

One day the ball fell in the river. One of his friends, Shridama insisted that Krishna should get his ball back. Despite the advices of other friends, Krishna leaped into the river. In there a terrible serpent, named Kaliya, used to reside. As soon as he saw Krishna, he opened his hood and started hissing. The poisonous breath of the snake turned Krishna's skin colour blue. This angered Krishna and he climbed upon the hood of Kaliya and started crushing his fangs. Thereafter the wives of the serpent begged Krishna to spare the life of their husband. Lord Krishna took pity upon them and came above the water while dancing on the hood of Kaliya and playing his flute. The residents of Gokul, who loved and adored Krishna immensely, were delighted upon seeing Krishna safe and stopped weeping since they had thought that Krishna was drowned in the river. The gods who witnessed the scene from the sky showered flowers and sang in the praise of Krishna.

6. **Gangavataran**—Bhagirath, the grandson of Suryavanshi King Anshuman , went out at a very young age to do penance for the salvation of the soul of his ancestors. After praying for one thousand years, Brahma was pleased and asked him to seek a boon. Bhagirath asked for two boons; the first being salvation for the souls of his ancestors who were burnt to ashes due to the curse of sage Kapil and the second that his lineage should continue.

Before the descent of Ganges on the earth, it was necessary to devise a way to block its rapid speed. For this purpose, Bhagirath prayed to Lord Shiva and pleased him. It is said that to set right the pride of Ganges, Shiva blocked Ganges for a long time in his Jatas (bun of hairs). At last Ganga prayed to Shiva and he released her from his jatas. Consequnetly, Ganga started flowing on the earth and as a result ancestors of Bhagirath achieved salvation and Bhagirath led Ganga on his superb chariot to the place where ashes of his ancestors were lying. Ganga is, therefore, called Bhagirathi as well.

7. **Govardhan Dharan**—Once Lord Krishna also known as 'Nandnandan' organised a prayer in the honour of Shri Giriraj (King of mountains). In this function all of the residents of Vraj and gods joined. However, successful completion of this prayer function angered Indra, the Lord of gods. He immediately summoned clouds called 'Sanvetak' and asked them to destroy Vraj.

On receipt of Indra's command, strange coloured clouds roared in anger and started raining. Along with heavy rains came tempest which uprooted the trees and houses. This terrified the residents of Vraj who came out of their houses and assembled in the Nandmandir (Nand's palace). They politely requested Krishna to guide them since it was at his suggestion they had stopped worshipping Indra and celebrated Govardhanpuja which angered Indra. Krishna, then advised the residents of Vraj to assemble near mountain Govardhan. Thereafter Krishna along with his people went to Govardhan and lifted it easily on his finger and protected the residents of Vraj from the anger of Indra. Everyone praised Krishna and gods showered beautiful flowers upon him.

8. **Gaj and Grah (The elephant and the crocodile)**—The elephant and crocodile were important kings in their previous life but because of a curse they were born as elephant and crocodile. Both of them were inimical to each other. One day when the elephant was drinking water from river Yamuna, the crocodile attacked it and pulled it below the water. Both fought fiercely with each other but when the elephant saw its life in peril and began to drown in the water he appealed to Lord Shri Hari for rescue. Hearing the elephant's pitiful cry, Lord Hari reached there along with other gods and severed the face of crocodile with his chakra and granted salvation to both of them.

9. **Tripurasur Vadh**—Once upon a time a demon named Tripurasur did penance and got a boon from Lord Shiva that he should not be defeated by anyone in battle. Lord Shiva while granting

the boon deposited his life in a pool of water and made a condition that the demon would not be defeated by anyone so long as there was water in the pool.

The grant of boon made Tripurasur wicked and he wanted to make Parvati his wife.

For a long time Shiva and Tripurasur fought with each other but the demon could not be defeated. Then Lord Shiva sought assistance from Brahma and Vishnu. Brahma and Vishnu transformed themselves as cow and calf respectively and drank entire water from the pool. Thereafter they sent Shiva to fight against the demon. In this way Shiva killed the demon and came to be known as 'Tripurari'

10. **Draupadi Cheer Haran**—Draupadi was married to the five Pandava brothers. Once chaupad, a game of gambling, was played between Pandavas and kauravas. Pandavas kept on betting whatever they had and lost. At the end they put Draupadi also on stake and lost.

Duryodhan who was the eldest of Kaurava brothers ordered Draupadi to be undressed in the full court to avenge an earlier insult. He commanded his younger brother, Dushasan, that Draupadi be brought to the court and undressed. On receiving the command, Dushasan went to the residence of Pandavas and told Draupadi that she has been won by them in chaupad and from then onwards she was to be their slave. Hearing this, Draupadi ran towards the harem of Dhritrashtra but Dushasan chased and dragged her by her hairs to the court and began to undress her. Draupadi aggrieved at her helpless condition started praying to Krishna in the following manner "Oh Govind, Oh Resident of Dwarka, Oh Sachhidanand! I am-sinking in the sea of Kaurvas, kindly protect me" she covered her face and started weeping.

Hearing the pitiful cries of Draupadi, Krishna immediately arrived there and secretly covered Draupadi with many beautiful sarees. Evil Dushasan made repeated attempts to pull Draupadi's sarees but as he pulled one saree after the other, the number of sarees went on increasing. Dushasan got tired and displeased with himself on his inability, sat in a corner of the court.

11. **Dashavatar (the ten incarnations of Lord Vishnu)**—Vishnu, to destroy the evil, took birth on the earth from time to time in different forms. Of these following ten incarnations of Vishnu are the most famous ones.

(i) *Matsyavatar* (As a fish)—During the dooms day, Vishnu was born as a fish in the sea and saved the mankind by taking Manu's boat to the highest point of the mountain.

(ii) *Kurmavatar* (As a tortoise)—Lord Vishnu appeared as a tortoise to bear the mountain of Mandar (Mandarachal) on his back to facilitate the stirring of sea by gods and demons.

(iii) *Shukaravatar* (As a boar)—Lord Vishnu was born as a boar and held earth on the front portion of his protruding teeth.

(iv) *Nrusinghavatar* (Half man Half Lion)—Vishnu appeared on the earth in half man half lion form and using his teeth and nails killed Harinya Kashyapu, the wicked king.

(v) *Wamanavatar* (As a pigmy)—Lord Vishnu assumed human form equal to the size of a thumb and deceived king Bali by seeking the universe for gods in grant.

(vi) *Parashuramavatar*—Lord Vishnu was born as Parashuram and killed all the kings who were responsible for the sins of the world.

(vii) *Ramavatar*—Lord Vishnu was born as Ram, son of Dashratha and killed the ten headed demon, Ravana.

(viii) *Krishnavatar*—Lord Vishnu was born as Krishna to kill evil kings like Kansa.

(ix) *Buddhavatar*—Lord Vishnu in his incarnation as Buddha preached truth, morality and non violence to the mankind.

(x) *Kalkiavatar*—This is yet to take place. At the end of Kaliyug Lord Vishnu will be born as a powerful child in house of a Brahman in the village Sambhal.

12. **Putanavadh**—King Kansa sent she demon Putana to Gokul with the object of killing child Krishna. On reaching Gokul, Putana transformed herself into a sixteen year old beautiful woman by using her magical powers. Her beauty put to shame even goddess like Saraswati, Laxmi, Rambha and Rati.

On entering the courtyard of Nand, Putana lifted the child Krishna in her arms and cuddling him put one of her breasts smeared with poison in his mouth. Shri Krishna was angered and he drank milk along with the life force of Putana.

When the she demon felt immense pain in her breasts, she ran out carrying Krishna in her arms and shouting "leave me, leave me." Her cries echoed through entire universe. On the other hand Nand and mother Yashoda were worried on account of disappearance of Krishna and all the residents of Vraj went out to search him. In deep forest they saw Krishna playing on the body of she demon. All the residents of Vraj and gods started praising the Lord.

13. **Panghat Leela** (Plays on the well)—Among many playful acts of Lord Krishna, Panghat Leela is very famous. Shri Krishna was very naughty in his childhood. When the cow herd maids (Gopis) went to the well to fill their pitchers with water Krishna used to play pranks with them. He often broke their pitchers or hid their robes or blocked their path. Krishna used to derive great pleasure from such pranks. Annoyed with pranks the cow herd maids used to abuse Krishna and complain to Yashoda. Mother Yashoda used to punish Krishna which was a matter of enjoyment for cow herd maids.

In Indian classical dances, the pranks of Krishna with cow maids form the most popular story line.

14. **Parvati Mangal**—The greatest of mountains which had many qualities was Himvan whose wife 'Maina' was the noblest woman of the three worlds. It was to Himvan and Maina, Parvati, the mother of world, was born.

When Parvati became mature her parents started worrying about her marriage and desired a suitable groom for Parvati.

One day sage Narad came to the house of Himvan when both husband and wife expressed their worry about a suitable groom for Parvati whereupon Naradji said that their daughter would get a half mad husband yet he would be worshipped by gods. Himvan and Maina were worried and enquired about ways to mitigate this defect. Then Naradji advised that Parvati should worship shiva.

From that day onwards Parvati engaged herself in worshipping Shiva but Shiva was not attracted by her youth and beauty. The gods, who wanted this marriage to be consummated, got together and made a plan. They sent cupid to Shiva but Shiva burnt him by glancing at the cupid from his third eye. Still Parvati did not give up her penance and began to eat Bel leaves instead of tubers and roots and after some time left eating them as well. At last one day to test her, Shiva, under the garb of a sage went to her and enquired the reason for such a hard penance. A friend of Parvati told him that Parvati desired to get Shiva as her husband. Upon hearing Parvati's desire, the sage said about Shiva that he lived upon alms, slept in crematorium, his food was cannabis and dhatura, covered himself with the ashes from crematorium and what she would get from such a husband. However, Parvati still remained firm on her choice. Upon knowing her views Shiva appeared in his true form and gratified her.

Shiva, thereafter, sent seven seers (saptarshis) to the house of Himvan to fix the date of marriage. On the appointed day, Shiva's marriage party which included gods as well as ghosts and demons, reached Himvan's house. Shiva himself was riding a bull. This strange marriage party caused a furore in the city and Parvati's mother Maina became unconscious. Himvan also became sad.

After enacting this drama, Shiva appeared in his grand and handsome form and his followers (ghosts and demons) also changed their form. Thereafter, the wedding of shiva and Parvati was performed with great pomp and show.

15. **Bhasmasur Vadh**—Once the demon Bhasmasur did extreme penance to please Shiva. Shiva, then, granted him the boon of his choice that one on whose head Bhasmasur kept his hand would be burnt to ashes. After getting the boon Bhasmasur's

intentions became bad and he first of all tried to put his hand on the head of Shiva.

Lord Shiva saw the danger and started to run and he was followed by Bhasmasur. When Lord Vishnu saw Shiva's condition he assumed the form of an extremely beautiful woman and started dancing on Bhasmasur's way with attractive gestures. Bhasmasur, seeing the dance of that bewitching woman, was attracted towards her whereupon that beautiful woman asked him to dance in the similar manner. Bhasmasur started to copy her and when during the dance, the woman put her hand on her head, Bhasmasur also did the same and was instantly burnt to ashes.

16. **Bhilni Bhakti**—Bhilni Shabri, an ardent devotee of Lord Rama, lived in a small hermitage in a forest. She worshipped Rama entire day. She had a strong belief that one day Rama would definitely come to her hermitage. During fourteen years of his banishment to forests, Rama sanctified the hermitages of many sages including that of Shabri. On getting a look of Lord Rama, Shabri was overjoyed and tears of love started flowing from her eyes.

She first prayed before Rama and thereafter brought some 'berries' from the forest as offering (bhog) for him. When she was picking berries in the forest she used to taste them and retained ones which were sweet and discarded others. Shabri offered sweet berries to the Lord and Rama ate them with great liking but Lakshman threw these berries behind himself as these had been already tasted by Shabri. Rama then explained to Laxman that he should not consider these berries as having been tasted before but appreciate the great devotion of Shabri.

17. **Makhan Leela**—Among the various playful acts of Lord Krishna, 'Makhan Leela' is the most famous one. Krishna liked butter from his childhood and along with his cowherd friends (Gwalas) he used to steal butter from the houses of cow herd maids (Gopies) and eat it.

When the cow herd maids did not find butter in their houses they complained to Yashoda that every day Krishna and his friends stole their butter and ate it. Hearing such complaints frequently,

Yashoda often punished Krishna and some times tied him to pestle or tied his hands and feet with a rope. Krishna used to explain to mother Yashoda that he was very small and his hands could not reach the ewer hanging from the roof. He mentioned that these cow maids were envious of him and made false accusations. Besides, there was no dearth of butter in his own house. Upon hearing such explanations, Yashoda became kindly disposed towards Krishna, embraced and fed butter to him with her own hands.

18. **Mareech Vadh**—Ravana, the King of Lanka, planned to kidnap Sita, the wife of Rama and sought assistance of Mareech in the matter. Ravana asked the Mareech to transform himself into a golden Deer and roam around Panchvati to disillusion Rama.

Mareech accepted the proposal of Ravana and began to roam around Panchvati in the form of a golden deer. When Sita suddenly saw this deer, she was attracted to it and insisted that Rama should kill the deer and bring its skin for her. Lord Rama followed the deer with his bow and arrows. The magical deer took Rama deep into forest and after going far Rama killed him with his arrow.

19. **Maharaas**—Maharaas is the gift of Krishna. It was upon the arrival of pleasant season on full moon day of Indian month of Kartik that the dance was performed by Lord Krishna along with cow herd maids (Gopis) with circular movements on the bank of river Yamuna at Vrindavan. This dance is known as Maha Raas.

Lord Krishna once on a full moon day of the month of Kartik had an urge to play Raas on the Bank of river Yamuna. He then played a very sweet tune on his flute hearing which the cow herd maids came out of their houses. Seeing that Krishna was playing on his flute, the cow herd maids began to dance with him and the Lord fulfilled their desire and between each of the two cow herd maids he placed himself (by taking many forms) and in this fashion performed the circular Raas.

During the course of Raas, the cow herd maids as well as Radha developed pride. Consequently, Lord Krishna immediately disappeared. With the sudden disappearance of the Lord, Radha and other cow herd maids started searching for him and weeping bitterly. They started saying to each other that they became proud as they performed Raas with Krishna and therefore, Krishna had disappeared. Then all the cow herd maids along with Radha immersed themselves in the fond memory of Lord Krishna and unified themselves into Krishna (Krishnakar). The Lord then reappeared and performed Raas for rest of the night.

20. **Madan Dahan**—Once cupid wanted to win the entire world and charmed it. Thereafter, cupid targeted Lord Shiva, arrived at the mountain Kailash and created the season of spring thereby making the entire atmosphere extremely pleasant.

At that time Lord Shiva was immersed in his meditation (Samadhi) but cupid fired his arrows upon him. This caused a break in Shiva's meditation and when he opened his eyes he saw the cupid behind a tree. Shiva was angered. He opened his third eye and burnt cupid by glancing at him.

When Lord Shiva heard the lamentation of Rati, the wife of cupid, he took pity on her and granted a boon that her husband would not die but remain alive without a body and would be known as 'Anang'

21. **Laxman Shakti**—After Ravana had kidnapped Sita, the wife of Rama, a great battle took place between the armies of Rama and Ravana. Ravana's army met with successive defeats. Then Ravana appointed his son Indrajit, as commander of the army and sent him to the battlefield. Indrajit Meghnad was very powerful and after fierce fighting defeated the Vanar Sena.

When Rama came to know about the condition of his army, he sent Laxman, his brother, to face Meghnad in the battlefield. Both of them fought for a long time and in the end Meghnad used a weapon named Veerghatini which was a type of Brahmastra and never failed. As a result Laxman was grievously hurt and became unconscious in the battlefield.

Meghnad and his soldiers made many attempts to lift Laxman but failed as Laxman was the incarnation of Sheshnag, the serpent who bears entire universe on his hood.

22. **Waman Avtar**—According to a mythological story, Maharaja Bali once became extremely proud of his fame and wealth. To rectify his pride, the omnipresent Lord assumed the form of a waman (pigmy) and went to his door asking for a piece of land equal to two and half times of Lord's step.

At that time Shukracharya who was guru of Bali advised him that the Waman was Lord Vishnu himself and had come to test him. However, the king considered himself to be a great provider and promised to give land equal to two and half times the step of waman. After the king made the promise, the Lord assumed a huge form and measured sky with one step and earth with second step and then asked Bali to provide for half step. The King then said that in two steps he had measured sky and earth and what else remained then. The king further said that for half a step he could take place from the king's body.

The Lord was pleased and disappeared stating that no one could retain pride.

23. **Vishwamitra Maneka**—Once the throne of Indra became unstable as Vishwamitra undertook a very hard penance. There was an outcry in the heaven and the gods became anxious.

At last it was decided that Vishwamitra's penance should be broken and for this Indra decided to use his nymphs. He sent the most beautiful nymph of his court to Vishwamitra. Maneka went to the hermitage of Vishwamitra and made provocative attempts to allure Vishwamitra. She brought spring season, danced in many ways and with her gestures deviated the mind of the sage from penance. As a result Vishwamitra's penance of many years became fruitless within a few moments.

24. **Surdas**—Surdas was a saraswat Brahmin. His father's name was Ramdas. He had taken up devotional music from his childhood. He was not born blind. He was a disciple of Shri Vallabhacharya and it was as per his command he used to sing the story of Bhagwat in musical poems (padas), In his collection 'Sursagar' the poems are based on the 10th chapter of Bhagwat.

It was the routine of Surdas to compose a new poem (pada) on his Lord Shri Nathji and sing it mellifluously, perform Kirtan and remain engrossed in singing about the qualities of the Lord.

In Sursagar the story of Lord Krishna beginning from birth to his return to Mathura has been rendered in great detail in the form of poems (padas). The poems in Sursagar are immersed in Shrinagar and Vatsalya rasas in a unique manner and it is not possible to find a parallel elsewhere. All padas composed by Surdas are unique.

25. **Sudama Leela**—Sudamaji was Shri Krishna's close friend while they were receiving education from sage Sandeepani. After the end of education both of them went to their respective homes. Lord Krishna became the king of kings and sudama lived his life in a dilapidated hut.

Once it so happened that successively for a few days Sudama's family had no food. Sudama's wife had her eyes wet with tears and thought that a person whose friend was the Lord himself, his children would be dying of hunger. She explained her feelings to Sudama. Sudama was extremely reluctant to go to Shri Krishna but at last he gave in and reached at his door enquiring his way from many a people. He had with him only four handful of rice.

As soon as the doorkeeper informed Shri Krishna of Sudama's arrival, he got up from his throne and ran to embrace Sudama. Tears started flowing from the eyes of both Krishna and Sudama.

Krishna took Sudama to Rukhmini and seated him respectfully. Krishna welcomed him very warmly. After some time Krishna asked Sudama, the gift that his sister-in-law (sudama's wife) would have sent for him. After considerable hesitation, Sudama gave the pouch containing the rice to Shri Krishna. Krishna ate two fistfuls of rice and when he was about to eat the third fistful, his wife Rukhmini stopped him and said that he had already given him the luxuries of two worlds and did he want to give her also. After enjoying the kingly pleasures with Shri Krishna for a few days, Sudama began his return journey. On reaching near his home, Sudama saw a beautiful palace in the place of his hut in which his wife and children were residing luxuriously.

As soon as Sudama's wife came to know about his arrival, she came out along with her friends to welcome him. Sudama was surprised to see all this and began to live comfortably.

26. **Sati Anusuiya**—Once sage Narad told Brahmani (wife of Brahma), Laxmi and Parvati that Anusuiya the wife of sage Atri was the most faithful one to her husband (pativrata). The three goddess became envious and sent their husbands to test Anusuiya. The three gods assumed the garb of a sage and went to Ansuiya seeking alms.

Anusuiya came to the door with alms and requested the sages to accept the same but three sages declined to accept unless Anusuiya gave the alms without wearing any clothes. At this request of sages, Anusuiya fell into a moral fix and started remembering her husband and praying that if three sages could become infants then this problem would get resolved. On the prayer of Anusuiya, the sages became three infants. Anusuiya took them in her hut and began to feed them without wearing any clothes.

About that time sage Atri returned to the hermitage after taking bath in river Ganges and found three infants lying in the crib. He was surprised and enquired about the infants. Anusuiya narrated the entire story.

When after a long time, the three gods did not return their wives became worried and reached the hermitage. They asked Anusuiya about their husbands who had gone there to test her. Anusuiya replied their husbands were lying in the crib and they could try to recognise and take them. At that time Atri could see the three gods through his internal eyes and requested them to assume their real form. The three gods did so and asked Atri and Anusuiya to ask the boon that they desired. Anusuiya requested that as her husband was required to walk great distance for taking bath in Ganges, the Lords should arrange to save him from this labour. Lord Vishnu thereupon pierced the earth with his arrow and caused Ganges to appear near the hermitage. This stream of Ganges is known as Vishnu Ganga.

2. TYPES OF MUSICAL INSTRUMENTS

From very early periods, various types of musical instruments have been in use in India. In 'Sangeet Ratnakar', written by Sharangdev, musical instruments have been divided into four main classes, *i.e.* 'Tatt', 'Sushir', 'Avandha' and 'Dhan'.

1. The instruments in which the tone is produced by using string or 'Tant' (gut), they are known as 'Tatt Vaadya' like Tanpura, Sarangi, Bela, Sitar, Sarod etc.
2. 'Sushir Vaadya' is that in which sound is produced by using controlled air circulation viz. Harmonium, Shehnai, Flute, Conch, Bugle, etc.
3. 'Avandha Vaadya' uses percussion for producing beats such as Tabla, Pakhavaj, Dholak, Damroo, Nagada, etc.
4. 'Ghan Vaadya' is that where sound is produced by using friction between two surfaces such as Manjeera, Jhanjh, Jal Tarang, etc.

In later paragraphs, main 'Tatta', 'Sushir', 'Avandha' and 'Ghan' instruments have been described in detail.

Tanpura

Tanpura is also called 'Tamboora'. It consists of a 'Tumba' of pumpkin. The 'Tumba' is cut from one side and a circular wooden piece is affixed. Further, a four and half feet long wooden rod is joined to the 'Tumba' and the wooden piece. At one end of this rod are four pegs and three steel and one brass wire are tied between these pegs and pegs at the base of the 'Tumba'. In some Tanpuras, there are two brass wires, one thick and one thin. On the circular wooden piece affixed to the 'Tumba' is a bridge structure and the four wires pass over it.

Tanpura is used for providing base tone for singing and playing other instruments.

Sitar

The main component of the Sitar is the 'Tumba' made of the pumpkin or round gourd. 'Tumba' is covered with a thin wooden lid on which 'Ghurach' etc. is placed; this lid is called 'Tabli'.

Upon the Tabli is placed a small platform made of bone or wood on which the wires of the Sitar pass and is called 'Ghurach'. At the end of the 'Tumba'there is an arrangement for tying wires. This arrangement is made by fixing pegs made of wood or bone. These pegs are called 'Langot' or 'Mongra' or 'Keel'.

Sitar has a long component fixed to the 'Tumba' which has pegs. This is called 'Dand'. The place where 'Tumba' and 'Dand' join each other is called 'Gul' or 'Gulu'. Close to the pegs are two strips made of bone or ivory. The wires pass on the strips through a hole which is called 'Taargahan'. The second strip on which the wires are placed is called 'Ati'.

On 'Dand', screens made of brass or iron are tied with thread or tant (gutwire). On placing fingers on the screen, various tones are produced. In the first wire of the Sitar, a pearl is placed between the 'Langot' and the "Gharuch' which is used for synchronizing the tones; this is called 'Manka' or 'Guriya'.

Sitar has seven pegs of wood for stretching wires. These pegs are used for tightening or loosening the wires.

Sarangi

Sarangi is a musical instrument made of wood of Sal or Jackfruit. Its length is approximately two and a quarter feet. Its head is broader than the base and is covered with hide. The lower part is covered with hide on both sides. It has three gut wires and others of steel. The wires are rubbed with a bow to produce musical tones.

Harmonium

Harmonium is a very popular musical instrument. This is played through 'Mathi'. It has metallic reeds and wooden strips. It has a box like structure and air is filled into it through 'Mathi'.

The air reaches the reeds through holes which can be opened or closed at will. When the holes are opened, air reaches these reeds and when the wooden strips are pressed, the air comes out of the reeds and produces musical tones. Harmonium is played solo also.

Flute

Flute is made of bamboo. The bamboo, which is used for making flute, is called 'Phulvansa'. It is approximately one and half to three feet long.

The hollow bamboo is closed from one side. Thereafter, the first hole is made 3 to 4 inches away from this end. This hole is used for blowing air into the flute. Approximately four inches down from the hole, 6 to 8 holes are made at definite intervals. The flute player moves his fingers over these holes while playing the flute and the air coming out of the holes produces musical notes.

Tabla

Tabla is used as an accompaniment while singing or playing other instruments. Tabla is of two types; (a) Right Tabla is a hollow piece made of wood covered with hide on the open end and (b) Left Tabla is again a hollow made of earth or metal with hide covering the open end. The various parts of the Right Tabla are described below :

1. *Tabla*—This is made of wood of Sheeshum, Jackfruit, Neem, Teak, and Sandalwood.
2. *Pudi*—The piece of hide, which covers the open end of the hollow wood, is called 'Pudi'. This is usually goatskin.
3. *Syaahi*—The black mixture deposited in the center of 'Pudi' is called 'Syaahi'.
4. *Chaanti*—On the circumference of Pudi, there is a double strip called 'Chaanti'.
5. *Maidaan*—The space between Chaanti and syaahi is called 'Maidan'.
6. *Gajra*—Around Pudi, there is a 'Gajra' made of hide which has holes. The 'Baddhi' (thong) is passed through the holes

and by striking at the 'Gajra', the Tabla is either tightened or brought down.

7. *Gatte*—There are eight wood pieces called 'Gatte' which are fixed at various places in 'Baddhi' for raising or bringing down the Tabla.
8. *Baddhi*—The leather thong, which is used for tightening the Pudi on Tabla, is called 'Baddhi'.
9. *Mundari*—On the base of the Tabla, a 'Mundari' is made of leather thong or thin rope. The 'Baddhi' is tightened through 'Mundari'.

The Left Tabla or 'Dagge' also has same components but is made up of earth or metal. Its circumference is larger than that of the Right Tabla. It, however, does not have 'Gatte' like the Right Tabla.

Procedure for synchronizing Tabla—For substantial raising or bringing down of the Tabla, 'Gatte's' are used and for minor adjustments a hammer is used for striking at the 'Gajra'. For raising the Tabla, the strike is made from the top and for bringing down, the strike is made from the base.

Pakhavaj

Pakhavaj is made by creating a hollow in wood of Sheeshum or Vijaysar and is slightly raised in the middle. Its right side is slightly smaller than the middle. Both sides are covered with hide.

In the right side, 'Syaahi' is applied and while playing, kneaded flour is applied on the left side. For joining the sides, a leather thong is used and wooden 'Gatta's' are placed under the thong.

Pair of Manjiras

Manjiras are made of brass or some other metal. By striking one manjira on the other, musical notes are produced. While playing them, open, closed and loud sounds can be produced as necessary.

3. KNOWLEDGE OF MUSICAL ASPECT

Swar

Swars are the musical notes. There are seven swars viz. Sa, Re, Ga, Ma, Pa, Dha, Ni. These are also known as Kshadaj, Rishabh, Gandhar, Madhyam, Pancham, Dhaiwat. Seven swars with 'Teevra Roop' are twelve but the basic swars are only seven.

Komal : When pure swar moves to lower than normal position, it is called 'Komal swar' viz. Re, Ga, Dha, Ni

Teevra : When pure swar rises upward from its appointed position it is called Teevra. Viz. Ma.

Shruti : Apart from the twelve swars of septet there are many other melodious sounds both above as well as below the swars which are called 'Shruti'.

Raag : This is a special composition of sound, which derive~ its beauty from 'Swars' and 'Varna'.

Thath : Thath is a special composition on swars in which all of the seven swars appear in an order.

Saptak : In music, basic pure swars are seven. These seven Swars reside in 'Saptak'. 'Saptaks' are of three types i.e. (1) Mandra Saptak, (2) Madhya Saptak and (3) Taar Saptak.

Varna : Apparent act of singing is called 'Varna'. There are four types viz. (1) Sthayee, (2) Arohi, (3) Avrohi and (4) Sanchari.

Sthayee : The first 'Pada' of poem is called 'Sthayee'.

Antara : The second 'Pada' of poem is called 'Antara'.

Sanchari : The third 'Pada' of the poem is called 'Sanchari'.

Aabhog : The last 'Pada' of poem is called 'Aabhog'.

Alankar : Regular composition of 'Varna' or special collection of swars is called 'Alankar'.

Aaroh-Avroh

While singing, the sound sometimes rises from one Swar to other and sometimes comes down from one Swar to other. This process is called Aaroh-Avroh.

Aalaap : Aalaap is taken before beginning the song. In 'Aalaap', without taking recourse to words, the 'raag' is demonstrated only with 'Aakaar', 'Eekaar' and 'Aikar'.

Dhwani (sound) : Whatever we hear in sound, the sound of singing, sobbing of a child and friction of two bricks are all examples of sound. However, we like to hear some sounds and dislike some. Music is related only to these sounds which are melodious and which we like to hear.

Naad

Regular and resonant melodious sound is called 'Naad'. In other words, musical sweet sound is 'Naad'. 'Naad' is the sound used in music which is regular and melodious. The sound which is irregular, unstable and unpleasant is not useful for music and cannot be called 'Naad'.

Peculiarities/Characteristics of 'Naad':

1. 'Naad' can be lower or higher: Sound which is created slowly is called 'Chota Naad' and if created rapidly is called 'Bada Naad '.
2. Height and Depth of 'Naad': Height and Depth of 'Naad' is dependent upon the frequency. If the frequency per second is higher, the 'Naad' is high (uncha) otherwise low (neecha).
3. The caste and quality of 'Naad's: Some learned men hold the view that 'Naad' is never alone but there are associated 'Naads' also. It is very difficult to recognize 'Associate Naads' distinctly only on hearing.

The number of 'Associate Naads' and their intensity is different for each instrument. Therefore, the sound of 'Bela' is different from Sitar, that of Sarangi is different from Tabla, and that of Harmonium is different from Sarod. This is called caste or quality of 'Naad'.

4. INTRODUCTION OF 'RAGAAS'

Raag Khamaj

This raag is based upon 'Khamaj Thaath'. In this raag both 'Nishad' and remaining pure 'swars' are used. In Aaroh pure 'Nishad' and Avroh 'Komal Nishad' is used and remaining swars are pure. 'Rishabh'is prohibited in 'Aaroh'. In 'Avroh' all the seven 'swars' are used and therefore its caste is 'Kshadav Sampoorna'.

Thath — Khamaj
Vadi — Gandhar
Time — Second quarter of night
Aaroh — Saa, Ga, Ma, Pa, Dha, Ni, Saa |
Avroh — Saa, Ni, Dha, Pa, Ma, Ga, Re, Saa |
Pakad — Ni, Dha, Pa, Ma, Dha, Ma, Ga |

Raag Bihag

In this raag, pure 'swars' are used. In the 'Aaroh'; 'Re' 'Dha' swars are prohibited and in the 'Avroh' all the seven swars are used and therefore its caste is 'Andav Sampoorna'. The 'Vadi Swar' is Gandhar and 'Sanvadi' is 'Nishad'. 'Alpa Teevra' is 'Ma' and remaining swars are pure.

Vadi — Gandhar Vilaval
Vadi — Gandhar
Time — First quarter of the night
Aaroh — Ni, Sa, Ga, Ma, Pa, Ni, Saa |
Avroh — Sa, Ni, Dha, Pa, Ma, Pa, Ga, Ma, Ga, Re, Sa |
Pakad — Ni, Sa, Ga, Ma, Pa, Ma, Pa, Ga, Ma, Ga, Re, Sa |

Raag Vilaval

In this raag all pure swars are used. In its 'Aaroh', 'Madhyam' is prohibited. In 'Avroh', seven swars are used. Therefore its caste is 'Kshadav Sampoorna'. 'Vadi Swar'is 'Dhaiwat' and 'Samwadi'is 'Gandhar'. Both 'Nishads' are used in 'Aaroh' and remaining swars are pure.

Thaath — Vilawal
Vadi — Dhaiwat
Time — First quarter of the day
Aaroh — Sa, Ga, Re, Ga, Pa, Dha, Ni, Saa |
Avroh — Sa, Ni, Dha, Pa, Dha, Ni, Dha, Pa, Ma, Ga, Ma, Re, Saa |
Pakad — Ga, Re S Ga, Pa, Ma, Ga, Ma, Re, Ga, Pa, Dha, Ni, Dha, Pa |

Raag Bhairavi

In this raag, 'Re' 'Ga' 'Dha' and 'Ni' arc soft swars. 'Madhyam'is 'vadi' and 'Kshadaj' is 'Samvadi'. Its caste is 'Sampoorna-Sampoorna'.

Thath — Bhairavi
Vadi — Madhyam
Time — Morning
Aaroh — Sa, Re, Ga, Ma, Pa, Dha, Ni, Saa |
Avroh — Sa, Ni, Dha, Pa, Ma, Ga, Re, Saa |
Pakad — Ma, Ga, Re, Ga, Saa, Re, Saa, Dha, Ni, Saa |

Raag Kafi

In this raag, 'Gandhar' and 'Nishad' are 'komal swars' (soft swars) and the remaining swars are pure. 'Pa' in 'vadi' and 'samvadi'. Its caste is 'Sampoorna-Sampoorna'.

Thath — Kafi
Vadi — Pancham
Time — Midnight
Aaroh — Saa, Re, Ga, Ma, Pa, Dha, Ni, Saa |
Avroh — Saa, Ni, Dha, Pa, Ma, Ga, Re, Saa |
Pakad — Saa, Saa, Re, Re, Ga, Ga, Ma, Pa |

Raag Tilak Kamod

In this raag, both 'Nishad' and the remaining pure swars are used. 'Vadi Swar'is 'Kshadaj' and 'Samvadi' is 'Pancham' in Aaroh, 'Gandhar' and 'Dhaiwat' swars are prohibited and in Avroh, 'Rishabh' is prohibited. Therefore, its caste is 'Andav—Khadav'.

Thath — Khamaj
Vadi — Pancham
Time — Second quarter of night
Aaroh — Saa, Re, Ga, Saa, Re, Ma, Pa, Dha, Ma, Pa, Saa |
Avroh — Saa, Re, Ga, Saa, Re, Ma, Pa, Dha, Ma, Pa, Saa |
Pakad — Pa, Ni, Saa, Re, Gaa, Saa, Re, Pa, Ma, Ga, Saa, Ni |

Raag Tilang

In this raag, 'Rishabh' and 'Dhaiwat' swars are prohibited and therefore its caste is 'Andav-Andav'. In the Aaroh, pure and in Avroh, komal 'Ni' are used. 'Samvadi'is 'Nishad'.

Thath — Khamaj
Vadi — Gandhar
Time — Second quarter of night
Aaroh — Saa, Gaa, Ma, Pa, Ni, Saa |
Avroh — Saa, Ni, Pa, Ma, Ga, Saa |
Pakad — Ni, Pa, Ga, Ma, Ga, Saa |

Raag Piloo

In this raag, pure and impure 12 swars of 'Saptak' are used. 'Komal Rishabh' and pure 'Gandhar' are used. 'Komal Dhaiwat' is used through 'Pancham'. 'Teevra Madhyam' is used sparingly. As 12 swars are used, its caste is 'Sankeerna'.

Thath — Kafi
Vadi — Gandhar
Time — Third quarter of the day
Aaroh — Ni, Saa, Ga, Re, Saa, Ga, Ma, Pa, Dha, Ma, Pa, Ni, Saa |
Avroh — Saa, Ni, Dha, Pa, Pa, Dha, Pa, Ga, Ma, Dha, Pa, Ga, Re, Saa, Ni, Saa |
Pakad — Ni, Saa, Ga, Re, Sa, Ni, Saa, Re, Saa, Ni, Dha, Pa, Ma, Pa, Ni, Maa |

Raag Desh

Both 'Nishads' are used in this raag. In the Aaroh, 'Gandhar' and 'Dhaiwat' are prohibited. In Avroh, all seven swars are used. Therefore, its caste is 'Andav Sampoorna'. In this raag, 'vadi' is 'Re' and 'Samvadi' is 'Pa'.

Thath — Khamaj
Vadi — Pancham
Time — Second quarter of night
Aaroh — Saa, Re, Ga, Pa, Ni, Saa |
Avroh — Saa, Ni, Dha, Pa, Ma, Ga, Re, Saa |
Pakad — Re, Ma, Pa, Ni, Dha, Pa, Pa, Dha, Pa, Ma, Ga, Re, Maa |

Raag Bahar

In its 'Aaroh' 'Re' and 'Avroh' 'Dha' are the prohibited swars and therefore its caste is 'Kshadav-Kshadav'. In this raag, 'Komal Gandhar' and both 'Nishads' are used. Vadi is 'Ma' and samwadi is 'Saa'.

Thath — Kafi
Vadi — Ma
Time — Midnight
Aaroh — Saa, Ma, Ma, Pa, Ga, Ma, Dha, Ni, Saa |
Avroh -- Saa, Ni, Pa, Ma, Pa, Ga, Ma, Re, Saa |
Pakad — Saa, Ma, Ma, Pa, Ga, Ma, Ni, Dha, Ni, Saa |

5. SINGING STYLES

Music is of two types (a) Margi and (b) Deshi.

Margi music is a creation of Gandharvas or Gods, the purpose of which is achievement of salvation. It is also called "Gandharva Music". Deshi music is for public entertainment. It is of two types (a) Taal Baddha (set on beats) and (b) Taal Rahit (without beats), Music set to beats is called "Nibaddha" and without beats is called" Anibaddha". "Anibaddha" music is of only one type *i.e.* "Alaap", "Nibaddha" music has several varieties such as "Dhrupad". "Dhamar", "Khayal", "Thumri" and "Lakshan Geet" etc. These are also called songs. The style of singing differentiates one song from the other. Whenever we hear a musician we can recognise the song on the basis of singing style *i.e.* whether he is singing Dhrupad or Khayal or something else. Some of the popular singing styles are described below.

Dhrupad—Dhrupad is an ancient singing style of India. It was created around 13th century A.D. In the court of Emperor Akbar, great singers sang only Dhrupad, Tansen was the greatest singers of these. Apart from Tansen, Singers like Swami Haridas Dagar, Nayak Baiju and Gopal etc. also used to render Dhrupad only.

Dhrupad is a serious singing style. Dhrupad singing puts more stress on throat and lungs and therefore it is also called male singing. The lyric is also of high order. Mostly the language of lyric has words from Braj, Hindi and Urdu. In this singing style Veer (bravery), Shant (peace) and Shringar (love) are the main rasas.

Dhrupad is sung in "Chartaal", "Teevra", "Sulfak", "Rudra", "Brahma" etc. taals. Mostly it has four components *i.e.* "Sthayee", "Antara", "Sanchari" and "Abhag". The singing is accompanied with "Pakhawaj". While singing initially there is an extended "Alaap" of "Nom Tom". In Dhrupad one can see enthralling "Layakaris".

Dhamar—It is also called "Hori" and is sung in "Dhamar" Taal. The lyric is related mostly to Holi, The lyric usually describes the playful acts of Radha-Krishna, Krishna and Cowherd Maids in the month of "Falgun". The languages are normally "Braj" and "Urdu" Dhamar singing also involves spectacular layakaris. Dhamar has two main components *i.e.* Sthayee and Antara. The chief Rasa is "Shringar".

Khayal—Khayal is a word of "Persian" language. It literally means the imagination or thought. The singer using his imagination and practice sings involving "Alaap", "Taan" and "Taal" etc. and this style is called "Khayal".

In this singing style, the singer has more freedom. Khayals are of two types :

(a) *Vilambit Khayal* : It is sung in "Vilambit Laya" and has two components, Sthayee and Antara. Its nature is serious. Use of "Murki", "Meend" , "Taan", "Palte", "Baltaan", "Bahlave" provides beauty to singing.

(b) *Drut Khayal* : The lyric is normally very short and has two components; Sthayee and Antara. The chief Rasas are Shringar and Karun. The singing style is akin to "Bada Khayal".

Tappa—Words of the lyric are mostly from Punjabi language. Its nature is "Chapal" (swift). It is sung in Ragas such as Kafi, Bhairavi, Piloo Desh, Khamaj and Jhinjhoti. The chief Rasa is Shringar. It has two components *i.e.* Sthayee and Antara. The singing style is different from others inasmuch as short and complex Taans are used. There is literally no "Alaap" and it requires a well groomed throat for singing Tappa.

This style of singing is more popular in Punjab and is sung in "Sitarkhani", "Phirodast" etc. Taals. It is said Ghulam Nabi Seri, invented this style of singing in the times of Muhammed Shah.

Bhajan—Bhajan is also a unique style of singing and is currently very popular. In this style not much emphasis is laid on the purity of Raag and the aim is to pray to the Lord. Usually

Keherwa, Dadra, Jhaptaal, Rupak, Teentaal etc. are the taals used in Bhajan singing. Devotion (Bhakti) is the main Rasa.

Holi—It is that style of singing which is often sung in "Kafi" Raag in "Deepchandi" Taal in the manner of a Thumri. The singing style is embellished with "Meend" , "Khatka" , "Kana", "Murki" etc.

Tarana—In Tarana singing the main Varnas (words) are Nom Tom, Tanan, Na Dir, Dir, Dani, Tadani etc. Tarana is sung in every Raag in almost all the Taals, it is gradually raised and reaches a crescendo before the end of singing.

The main aim of Tarana singing is preparation, layakari and pronunciation practice. More often, the singers render Tarana after "Chota Khayal"

Ghazal—The song is usually composed in "Urdu" or "Persian. Its nature is considered "Kshudra" (inferior). Ghazal is usually rendered in same Raga as Thumri, Tappa etc. Shringar is main Rasa. The "Taals" commonly used are Deepchandi, Dadra, Teevra or Paston etc. The poem has many Antaras, Attention is paid to the purity of Raga.

Thumri—It is that style of singing where more importance is given to beauty of "Bhavas" than to purity of Raga. The origin of word Thumri is from "Thumka" (dance). This style of singing is meant for dancing. According to some learned persons the origin of Thumri can be traced to 17th, 18th and beginning of 19th Centruy.

Thumri is of two types (i) Thumari of "Bol Banava" and (ii) Thumari of "Bol Baant". Thumari of "Bol Banava" is mostly sung in Teen Taal as Vilambit Laya involving Deepchandi or Punjabi Theka. Thumri of "Bol Baant" type is sung in "Madhya Laya" in Teen Taal and in these Thumris the smartness of Laya is evident.

Thumris are mainly based on Shringar Rasa and Nayika bhed, Main Language is Urdu but at times" Avadhi" influence can also be seen.

In Thumri singing not much emphasis is laid upon purity of Raga. The singers (male as well as female) mix various Ragas to add melody to singing. Punjabi, Deepchandi, Teen Taal, Keherwa etc. are the Taals used in this style of singing.

Thumri developed in Lucknow during the reign of Wazid Ali Shah. He himself composed many Thumris under the pseudonym "Akhtar Piya". He had appointed many great dancers to his court to demonstrate "Bhavas" on his Thumris. He created a dance drama "Raas" and "Indersabha" in which Thumris were used for singing and enacting of female roles.

6. BHATKANDE OR VISHNUDIGAMBER TAL NOTATION

	BHATKANDE Paddhiti	VISHNUDIGAMBER Paddhiti
SAM	X	|
KHALI	O	+
TALI	NUMBERS OF TALS 2, 3, ETC.	NUMBERS OF MATRAS 5,13 NO.VIBHAGA AFTER EACH ROUND, A LINE IS GENERALLY DRAWN.

MATRA PERIOD

ONE MATRA Ta	NO MARK	Ta
1½ MATRAS	Ta — Ta	Ta O Ta o
2 MATRAS	Ta —	Ta " ~
3 MATRAS	Ta — —	Ta o
4 MATRAS	Ta — — —	Ta X
HALF MATRA	Tat Tat	Ta Ta Ta Ta O O O O
1/4 MATRA	Thei Tat	Th Ei Ta Ta
1/3 MATRA	Ta Tae Te	Ta Tae Te 1/3 1/3 1/3
1/6 MATRA	Dhig Dhig Dhig	Dhi Ga Dhi Ga Dhi Ga 1/6 1/6 1/6 1/6 1/6 1/6
ARDHAVIRAM	Ta, Tat	NO ARDHAVIRAM

Ta = 1/2, Ta [illegible] 1/[illegible] [illegible]a = 1/4

7. TYPES OF 'TAAL' FORMATIONS IN NORTH AND SOUTH INDIA

The present form of Indian Music is distinguished in two parts viz. North Indian or Hindustani Classical music and South Indian or Carnatic music.

Types of formation of *'Taal'* in North Indian Music

The formations of *'taal'* in North Indian Music are based on the ancient cultural methods. The only difference between the taal formations of old classical music and Hindustani classical music today are in the types of 'kriyas' as worded or non-worded. The other dependable factors of the taal (10 'prans') are used for creativity and other factors like Grah, Jaati, Laya and Prastaar give a new meaning to the taal which leads to new horizons in the taal formation. This is why new forms of *taal* with new and different speed levels take birth in North India.

The formation of *taal* in northern India is based on a very simple principle. Firstly, a *'maatra'* is kept firm in the *taal* formation. Then according to the increasing and decreasing speed levels, the *taal* is divided into several parts. Then to make this formation of *taal* more specific the positions of the *'taali"* and the *'khaali"* are assigned to the *taal* formation. There is always a *taali* on the very first *maatra* of the *taal* and this *taali* is called *'sama'*. There can be two, three or more *taalis* in the formation of the *taal* but there is always a *khaali* between every two *taalis*. There can never be two or three *khaalis* consecutively in the formation of the *taal.* According to some learned men, *khaali* is an imagination made to correctly signify the position of the *sama.* A *khaali* is always kept in the middle of the *taal.* Some examples of these kind of *taals* are—Teentaal, Keherwa, Daadra, Jhaptaal, etc. If the taal is odd numbered, the 'khaali' is placed only after completing the first half of the taal. *e.g.* Panchamswari.

Therefore, it is clearly visible that the method of taal formation in north India is based on the principles written down in the old books but has seen changes according to the changing times.

Types of '*taal*' formation in South India

In ancient times, old cultural methods were used in the formation of *taal* in south India but during the Dark Ages, all these methods got lost and a *'Salagsood'* named source was made available which consisted of seven *taals* which came to use in the *taal* formations in south India. These are stated below :—

1. Dhrava – 1011 2. Mathya – 101 3. Rupak – 01
4. Jhampa – 10 5. Triputa – 100 6. Addad – 1100
7. Ektaal – 1

After viewing the formations of these above stated *taals,* the following characteristics are realised —

1. in these *taals,* the three bodies of formation of *taal, 'Anudrata', 'Drata'* and *'Laghu'* are brought to use.
2. *'Laghu'* is used in every formation of the *taal.*
3. In *Dhruva, Mathya* and *Addad,* there is one and can be more *'Laghu'*s added in the formation of the *taal.*
4. The *taal* formation of *Dhruva* and *Addad* is divided in 4 parts; *'Mathya', Jhampa'* and *'Triputa'* are divided in 3 parts; *'Rupak' in* 2 parts and *'Ektaal' has only one part.*

In Carnatic music, when the existing seven *taals* were not found to be sufficient for making more new formations of *taals,* then 5 types of every *taal* were taken as base to form 5 sub-parts of the existing 7 *taals.* This way 7x5=35 formations of *taal* are in use presently. They are all used in *'Laghu'* respecting the old tradition.

If there is a *maatra,* it becomes *'Anudrata'* (1/4) and *'Drata'* (1/2) and according to the types of formation of *taal*, performing it 5 times, 7 times or more, it does not make any difference as it comes to its intended ending number. That is why in this form of art, some rules which were essential were made. Firstly, every body of the taal should be made 4 times so that *Laghu* comes to its

4 *maatra, Drata* comes to 2 and *Anudrata* comes to one. Based on the other factors, change in the number of the 'maatra' results in a change in 'Laghu maatra' and the other parts of the taal will remain same as before.

In this manner, the 7 taal formations in Carnatic music are divided into their 5 sub-parts which are listed as under:

TYPE	Parts of maatra	Total maatras
1. Dhruva Taal	Form - 1011	
(a) Tryastra	3+2+3+3	= 11
(b) Chatustra	4+2+4+4	= 14
(c) Khanda	5+2+5+5	= 17
(d) Mishra	7+2+7+7	= 23
(e) Sankirna	9+2+9+9	= 29
2. Madhya Taal	Form - 101	
(a) Tryastra	3+2+3	= 8
(b) Chatustra	4+2+4	= 10
(c) Khanda	5+2+5	= 12
(d) Mishra	7+2+7	= 16
(e) Sankirna	9+2+9	= 20
3. Rupak Taal	Form - 01	
(a) Tryastra	2+3	= 5
(b) Chatustra	2+4	= 6
(c) Khanda	2+5	= 7
(d) Mishra	2+7	= 9
(e) Sankirna	2+9	= 11
4. Jhampa Taal	Form - 10	
(a) Tryastra	3+ 1 +2	= 6
(b) Chatustra	4+ 1 +2	= 7
(c) Khanda	5+1+2	= 8
(d) Mishra	7+1+2	= 10
(e) Sankirna	9+1+2	= 12

5. Triputa Taal	Form - 101	
(a) Tryastra	3+2+2	= 7
(b) Chatustra	4+2+2	= 8
(c) Khanda	5+2+2	= 9
(d) Mishra	7+2+2	= 11
(e) Sankirna	9+2+2	= 13
6. Addad Taal	Form - 1100	
(a) Tryastra	3+3+2+2	= 10
(b) Chatustra	4+4+2+2	= 12
(c) Khanda	5+5+2+2	= 14
(d) Mishra	7+7+2+2	= 18
(e) Sankirna	9+9+2+2	= 22
7. Ektaal	Form - 1	
(a) Tryastra	3	
(b) Chatustra	4	
(c) Khanda	5	
(d) Mishra	7	
(e) Sankirna	9	

Other than the above stated taal formations, during the nine 'Sandhi Kaal'. In the seva-pooja (offerings) in the temples of South India, the 9 taals in which the devotional songs were sung are known as the 'Nava Sandhi Taal'. They are as under—

Name of Sandhi	Name of Taal	Body ofTaal
1. Bhrama Sandhi	Bhrama	1S1S
2. Indra Sandhi	Indra	11S100
3. Agni Sandhi	Mattayan	10101
4. Yama Sandhi	Bhrungi	IS11
5. Niraruti	Niraruti	111100
6. Varun Sandhi	Nava	10001
7. Vayu Sandhi	Bali	0001
8. Kuber Sandhi	Kottari	SSS
9. Eeshaan Sandhi	Tannkiri	SIS

in this manner, the types of taal formations in south Indian music are small and easily and clearly understandable. That is why it is looked upon with great interest and respect.

8. A COMPARATIVE STUDY OF TAAL SYSTEM IN KARNATIC AND HINDUSTANI STYLE

(1) In the Karnatic style there are thirty five Taals but there are no limitation on Taals in Hindustani style.

(2) In the Karnatic style there are 7 main taals. The 35 taals comprise 5 Jatis and the matras of **Lagher** are 4, 3, 7 and 5 respectively and their combination add upto thirty five but it is not so in Hindustani style.

(3) Both styles have different scripts for notation.

(4) Today in the Karnatic style signs like Laghu, Guru, Plut, Drut and Anudrut are seen but in Hindustani Taal System names of signs are not used.

(5) In Hindustani Taal system, Taal has 10 (ten) characteristics, Sevaryukt bol, Paran etc, which are the basis of Taal system, the same are considered as basis for Karnatic Taal style.

(6) The medium for playing Hindustani Taals is mostly Tabla Dagga but Karnataki Taal is played on Ghatam *i.e.* an earthern pitcher.

(7) The Jati's are considered more important in Hindustani Taal style than Karnatic.

(8) The Bolakshars of Hindustani Taals are based on Bols of ancient Mrudang playing viz. Ka, Kha, Ga, Gha, Ta, Tha, Da, Dha, Ta, Tha, Da, Dha, Da, Ra, Ra, Ha totalling sixteen. However, in Karnatic style the Bolakshars are not based on ancient Mrudang play.

(9) There is no sign indicated for 'Khali' in Karnatic Taal style but silent Paat kriya, Avat, Nishkrum, Vikshep and Pravesh actions are expressed through definite hand gestures. However, in Hindustani style there is sign for Khali.

(10) In both Karnatic and Hindustani style, the medium for playing Taals being different, the style of playing Taals is found to be different.

●●●

6

PRACTICAL PART

1. THAH, DUGUN, TUGUN, CHOWGUN OF DIFFERENT TAALS

DADARA

MAATRA – 6, VIBHAGA – 2, TALI – 1, KHALI – 1

THAH	1 DHA X	2 DHI	3 NA
	4 DHA 0	5 TI	6 NA
DUGUN	1 DHADHI X	2 NADHA	3 TINA
	4 DHADHI 0	5 NADHA	6 TINA
TUGUN	1 DHADHINA X	2 DHATINA	3 DHADHINA
	4 DHATINA 0	5 DHADHINA	6 DHATINA

CHOWGUN	1	2	3
	DHADHINADHA	TINADHADHI	NADHATINA
	X		
	4	5	6
	DHADHINADHA	TINADHADHI	NADHATINA
	0		

TAAL TEEVRA

MAATRA – 7, VIBHAGA – 3, TAALI – 3

THAH	1	2	3
	DHA	DIN	TA
	X		
	4	5	6
	TIT	KAT	GADI
	2		3
	7		
	GAN		
DUGUN	1	2	3
	DHADIN	TATIT	KATGADI
	X		
	4	5	6
	GANDHA	DINTA	TITKAT
	2		3
	7		
	GADIGAN		
TUGUN	1	2	3
	DHADHINTA	TITKATGADI	GANDHADHIN
	X		
	4	5	6
	TATITKAT	GADIGANDHA	DHINTATIT
	7		3
	KATGADIGAN		
CHOWGUN	1	2	3
	DHADHINTATIT	KATGADIGANDHA	DINTATITKAT
	X		
	4	5	6
	GADIGANDHADIN	TATITKATGADI	GANDHADINTA
	2		3
	7		
	TITKATGADIGAN		

RUPAK TAAL

MAATRA – 7, VIBHAGA – 3, TAALI – 2, KHALI – 1

THAH	1	2	3
	TIN	TIN	NA
	X		
	4	5	6
	DHI	NA	DHI
	2		0
	7		
	NA		
DUGUN	1	2	3
	TINTIN	NADHI	NADHI
	X		
	4	5	6
	NATIN	TINNA	DHINA
	2		0
	7		
	DHINA		
TUGUN	1	2	3
	TINTINNA	DHINADHI	NATINTIN
	X		
	4	5	6
	NADHINA	DHINATIN	TINNADHI
	2		0
	7		
	NADHINA		
CHOWGUN	1	2	3
	TINTINNADHI	NADHINATIN	TINNADHINA
	X		
	4	5	6
	DHINATINTIN	NADHINADHI	NATINTINNA
	2		0
	7		
	DHINADHINA		

TAAL DHUMAALI

MAATRA – 8, VIBHAGA – 4, TAALI – 3, KHALI - 1

THAH

1	2	3
DHA	DHIN	DHA
X		2
4	5	6
TIN	TAK	DHIN
	0	
7	8	
DHAGE	TIRKIT	
3		

DUGUN

1	2	3
DHADHIN	DHATIN	TAKDHIN
X		2
4	5	6
DHAGETIRKIT	DHADHIN	DHATIN
	0	
7	8	
TAKDHIN	DHAGETIRKIT	
3		

TUGUN

1	2	3
DHADHINDHA	TINTAKDHIN	DHAGETIRKITDHA
X		2
4	5	6
DHINDHATIN	TAKDHINDHAGE	TIRKITDHADHIN
	0	
7	8	
DHATINTAK	DHINDHAGETIRKIT	
3		

CHOWGUN	1	2
	DHADHINDHATIN	TAKDHINDHAGETIRKIT
	X	
	3	4
	DHADHINDHATIN	TAKDHINDHAGETIRKIT
	2	
	5	6
	DHADHINDHATIN	TAKDHINDHAGETIRKIT
	0	
	7	8
	DHADHINDHATIN	TAKDHINDHAGETIRKIT
	3	

TAAL KEHERWA

MAATRA – 8, VIBHAGA – 2, TAALI – 1, KHALI – 1

THAH	1	2	3	4
	DHA	GE	NA	TI
	X			
	5	6	7	8
	NA	KA	DHI	NA
	0			
DUGUN	1	2	3	4
	DHAGE	NATI	NAKA	DHINA
	X			
	5	6	7	8
	DHAGE	NATI	NAKA	DHINA
	0			

TUGUN	1	2	3
	DHAGENA	TINAKA	DHINADHA
	X		
	4	5	6
	GENATI	NAKADHI	NADHAGE
		0	
	7	8	
	NATINA	KADHINA	
CHOWGUN	1	2	3
	DHAGENATI	NAKEDHINA	DHAGENATI
	X		2
	4	5	6
	NAKEDHINA	DHAGENATI	NAKEDHINA
		0	
	7	8	
	DHAGENATI	NAKEDHINA	

BASANT TAAL

MAATRA – 9, VIBHAGA- 9, TAALI – 6, KHALI – 3

THAH

1	2	3	4
DHA	DI	TA	GHE
X	2	3	4
5	6	7	8
TA	TIT	KAT	GADI
0	5	0	6
9			
GAN			
0			

DUGUN

1	2	3	4
DHADI	TAGHE	TATIN	KATGADI
X	2	3	4
5	6	7	8
GANDHA	DITA	GHETA	TITKAT
0	5	0	6
9			
GADIGAN			
7			

TUGUN

1	2	3
DHADITA	GHETATIT	KATGADIGAN
X	2	3
4	5	6
DHADHITA	GHETATIT	KATGADIGAN
4	0	5
7	8	9
DHADITA	GHETATIT	KATGADIGAN
0	6	0

CHOWGUN	1	2	3
	DHADITAGHE	TATITKATGADI	GANDHADITA
	X	2	3
	4	5	6
	GHETATITKAT	GADIGANDHADHI	TAGHETATIT
	4	0	5
	7	8	9
	KATGADIGANDHA	DITAGHETA	TITKATGADIGAN
	0	6	7

SHOOL TAAL

MAATRA – 10, VIBHAGA – 2, TAALI – 3, KHALI – 1

THAH

1	2	3	4
DHA	DHA	DHIN	TA
X		0	
5	6	7	8
KIT	DHAGE	TIT	KAT
2		3	
9	10		
GADI	GAN		
0			

DUGUN

1	2	3	4
DHADHA	DHINTA	KITDHAGE	TITKAT
X		0	
5	6	7	8
GADIGAN	DHADHA	DHINTA	KITDHAGE
2		3	
9	10		
TITKAT	GADIGAN		
0			

TUGUN

1	2	3
DHADHADHIN	TAKITDHAGE	TITKATGADI
X		0
4	5	6
GANDHADHA	DHINTAKIT	DHAGETIRKIT
	2	
7	8	9
GADIGANDHA	DHADHINTA	KITDHAGETIT
3		0
10		
KATGADIGAN		

CHOWGUN

1	2
DHADHADHINTA	KITDHAGETITKAT
X	
3	4
GADIGANDHADHA	DHINTAKITDHAGE
0	
5	6
TITKATGADIGAN	DHADHADHINTA
2	
7	8
KITDHAGETITKAT	GADIGANDHADHA
3	
9	10
DHINNAKITDHAGE	TITKATGADIGAN
0	

JHAPTAAL

MAATRA – 10, VIBHAGA – 4, TAALI – 3, KHALI – 1

THAH	1	2	3	4
	DHI	NA	DHI	DHI
	X		2	
	5	6	7	8
	NA	TI	NA	DHI
		0		3
	9	10		
	DHI	NA		
DUGUN	1	2	3	4
	DHINA	DHIDHI	NATI	NADHI
	X		2	
	5	6	7	8
	DHINA	DHINA	DHIDHI	NATI
		0		3
	9	10		
	NADHI	DHINA		
TUGUN	1	2	3	4
	DHINADHI	DHINATI	NADHIDHI	NATINA
	X		2	
	5	6	7	8
	DHIDHINA	DHINADHI	DHINATI	NADHIDHI
		0		3
	9	10		
	NATINA	DHIDHINA		

CHOWGUN	1	2	3
	DHINADHIDHI	NATINADHI	DHINADHINA
	X		2
	4	5	6
	DHIDHINATI	NADHIDHINA	DHINADHIDHI
			0
	7	8	9
	NATINADHI	DHINADHINA	DHIDHINATI
		3	
	10		
	NADHIDHINA		

ASHTA MANGAL TAAL

MAATRA – 11, VIBHAGA – 11, TAALI – 8, KHALI – 3

THAH

1	2	3	4
DHIN	NA	DHIN	DHIN
X	0	2	3
5	6	7	8
NA	DHIN	DHIN	NA
0	4	5	0
9	10	11	
DHAGE	NADHA	TAK	
6	7	8	

DUGUN

1	2	3
DHINNA	DHINDHIN	NADHIN
X	0	2
4	5	6
DHINNA	DHAGENADHA	TAKDHIN
3	0	4
7	8	9
NADHIN	DHINNA	DHINDHIN
5	0	6
10	11	
NADHAGE	NADHATAK	
7	8	

TUGUN

1	2	3
DHINNADHIN	DHINNADHIN	DHINNADHAGE
X	0	2
4	5	6
NADHATAKDHIN	NADHINDHIN	NADHINDHIN
3	0	4

7	8	9
NADHAGENADHA	TAKDHINNA	DHINDHINNA
5	0	6

10	11
DHINDHINA	DHAGENADHATAK
7	8

CHOWGUN

1	2
DHINNADHINDHIN	NADHINDHINNA
X	0
3	4
DHAGENADHATAKDHIN	NADHINDHINNA
2	3
5	6
DHINDHINNADHAGE	NADHATAKDHINNA
0	4
7	8
DHIDHINNADHIN	DHINNADHAGENADHA
5	0
9	10
TAKDHINNADHIN	DHINNADHINDHIN
6	7
11	
NADHAGENADHATAK	
8	

CHOUTAAL

MAATRA – 12, VIBHAGA – 6, TAALI – 4, KHALI – 2

THAH

1	2	3	4
DHA	DHA	DHIN	TA
X		0	
5	6	7	8
KIT	DHAGE	DIN	TA
2		0	
9	10	11	12
TIT	KAT	GADI	GAN
3		4	

DUGUN

1	2	3
DHADHA	DHINTA	KITDHAGE
X		0
4	5	6
DINTA	TITKAT	GADIGAN
	2	
7	8	9
DHADHA DHINTA	KITDHAGE DINTA	TITKAT
0	3	4
10		
GADIGAN		

TUGUN

1	2	3
DHADHADHIN	TAKITDHAGE	DINTAKIT
X		0
4	5	6
KATGADIGAN	DHADHADHIN	TAKITDHAGE
	2	
7	8	9
DINTAKIT	KATGADIGAN	DHADHADHIN
0		3
10	11	12
TAKITDHAGE	DINTAKIT	KATGADIGAN
	4	

CHOWGUN

1	2
DHADHADHINTA	KITDHAGEDINTA
X	
3	4
TITKATGADIGAN	DHADHADHINTA
0	
5	6
KITDHAGEDINTA	TITKATGADIGAN
2	
7	8
DHADHADHINTA	KITDHAGEDINTA
0	
9	10
TITKATGADIGAN	DHADHADHINTA
3	
11	
KITDHAGEDINTA	TITKATGADIGAN
4	

EKTAAL

MAATRA – 12, VIBHAGA – 6, TAALI – 4, KHAALI – 2

THAH				
	1	2	3	4
	DHIN	DHIN	DHAGE	TIRKIT
	X		0	
	5	6	7	8
	TU	NA	KAT	TA
	2		0	
	9	10	11	12
	DHAGE	TIRKIT	DHI	NA
	3		4	

DUGUN			
	1	2	3
	DHINDHIN	DHAGETIRKIT	TUNA
	X		0
	4	5	6
	KATTA	DHAGETIRKIT	DHINA
		2	
	7	8	9
	DHINDHIN	DHAGETIRKIT	TUNA
	0		3
	10	11	12
	KATTA	DHAGETIRKIT	DHINA

TUGUN		
	1	2
	DHINDHIDHAGE	TIRKITTUNA
	X	
	3	4
	KATTADHAGE	TIRKITDHINA
	0	
	5	6
	DHINDHINDHAGE	TIRKITTUNA
	2	

7	8
KATTADHAGE	TIRKITDHINA
0	
9	10
DHINDHINDHAGE	TIRKITTUNA
3	
11	12
KATTADHAGE	TIRKITDHINA
4	

CHOWGUN

1	2
DHINDHINDHAGETIRKIT	TUNAKATTA
X	
3	4
DHAGETIRKITDHINA	DHINDHINDHAGETIRKIT
0	
5	6
TUNAKATTA	DHAGETIRKITDHINA
2	
7	8
DHINDHINDHAGETIRKIT	TUNAKATTA
0	
9	10
DHAGETIRKITDHINA	DHINDHINDHAGETIRKIT
3	
11	12
TUNAKATTA	DHAGETIRKITDHINA
4	

DHAMAAR TAAL

MAATRA – 14, VIBHAGA – 4, TAALI – 3, KHALI – 1

THAH	1	2	3	4
	KA	DHI	TA	DHI
	X			
	5	6	7	8
	TA	THA	S	GA
		2		0
	9	10	11	12
	TIT	TA	TI	TA
			3	
	13	14		
	TA	S		
DUGUN	1	2	3	4
	KADHI	TADHI	TATHA	S GA
	X			
	5	6	7	8
	TITTA	TITA	TA S	KADHI
		2		0
	9	10	11	12
	TADHI	TATHA	S GA	TITTA
			3	
	13	14		
	TITA	TA S		
TUGUN	1	2	3	4
	KADHITA	DITATHA	S GATIT	TATITA
	X			
	5	6	7	8
	TA S KA	DHITADHI	TATHA S	GATITTA
		2		0
	9	10	11	12
	TITATA	S KADHI	TADHITA	THA S GA
			3	
	13	14		
	TITTATI	TATA S		

CHOWGUN

1	2	3
KADHITADHI X	TATHA S GA	TITTATITA
4	5	6
TA S KADHI	TADHITATHA	S GATITTA 2
7	8	9
TITATA S	KADHITADHI 0	TATHA S GA
10	11	12
TITTATITA	TA S KADHI 3	TADHITATHA
13	14	
S GATITTA	TITATA S	

TAAL PANCHAM SAWARI

MAATRA – 15, VIBHAGA – 4, TAALI – 3, KHALI – 1

THAH

1	2	3	4
DHI	NA	DHIDHI	KAT
X			2
5	6	7	8
DHIDHI	NADHI	DHINA	TIRKIT
			0
9	10	11	12
TUNA	TIRKIT	TUNA	KATTA
			3
13	14	15	
DHIDHI	NADHI	DHINA	

DUGUN

1	2	3
DHINA	DHIDHIKAT	DHIDHINADHI
X		
4	5	6
DHINATIRKIT	TUNATIRKIT	TUNAKATTA
2		
7	8	9
DHIDHINADHI	DHINADHI	NADHIDHI
	0	
10	11	12
KATDHIDHI	NADHIDHINA	TIRKITTUNA
		3
13	14	15
TIRKITTUNA	KATTADHIDHI	NADHIDHINA

TUGUN

1	2
DHINADHIDHI	KATDHIDHINADHI
X	
3	4
DHINATIRKITTUNA	TIRKITTUNAKATTA
	2

5	6
DHIDHINADHIDHINA	DHINADHIDHI
7	8
KATDHIDHINADHI	DHINATIRKITTUNA
	0
9	10
TIRKITTUNAKATTA	DHIDHINADHIDHINA
3	
11	12
DHINADHIDHI	KATDHIDHINADHI
	3
13	14
DHINATIRKITTUNA	TIRKITTUNAKATTA
15	
DHIDHINADHIDHINA	

CHOWGUN

1	2
DHINADHIDHIKAT	DHIDHINADHIDHINATIRKIT
X	
3	4
TUNATIRKITTUNAKATTA	DHIDHINADHIDHINADHI
	2
5	6
NADHIDHIKATDHIDHI	NADHIDHINATIRKITTUNA
7	8
TIRKITTUNAKATTADHIDHI	NADHIDHINADHINA
	0
9	10
DHIDHIKATDHIDHINADHI	DHINATIRKITTUNATIRKIT
11	12
TUNAKATTADHIDHINADHI	DHINADHINADHIDHI
	3
13	14
KATDHIDHINADHIDHINA	TIRKITTUNATIRKITTUNA
15	
KATDHIDHINADHIDHINA	

TEENTAAL

MAATRA – 16, VIBHAGA – 4, TAALI – 3, KHAALI – 1

THAH

1	2	3	4
DHA	DHIN	DHIN	DHA
X			
5	6	7	8
DHA	DHIN	DHIN	DHA
2			
9	10	11	12
DHA	TIN	TIN	TA
0			
13	14	15	16
TA	DHIN	DHIN	DHA
3			

DUGUN

1	2	3
DHADHIN	DHINDHA	DHADHIN
X		
4	5	6
DHINDA	DHATIN	TINTA
	2	
7	8	9
TADHIN	DHINDHA	DHADHIN
		0
10	11	12
DHINDHA	DHADHIN	DHINDHA
13	14	15
DHATIN	TINTA	TADHIN
3		
16		
DHINDHA		

TUGUN

1	2	3
DHADHINDHIN	DHADHADHIN	DHINDHADHA
X		

4 TINTINTA
5 TADHINDHIN
2
6 DHADHADHIN

7 DHINDHADHA
8 DHINDHINDHA
9 DHATINTIN
0

10 TATADHIN
11 DHINDHADHA
12 DHINDHINDHA

13 DHADHINDHIN
3
14 DHADHATIN
15 TINTATA

16 DHINDHINDHA

CHOWGUN

1 DHADHINDHINDHA
X
2 DHADHINDHINDHA

3 DHATINTINTA
4 TADHINDHINDHA

5 DHADHINDHINDHA
2
6 DHADHINDHINDHA

7 DHATINTINTA
8 TADHINDHINDHA

9 DHADHINDHINDHA
0
10 DHADHINDHINDHA

11 DHATINTINTA
12 TADHINDHINDHA

13 DHADHINDHINDHA
3
14 DHADHINDHINDHA

15 DHATINTINTA
16 TADHINDHINDHA

SHIKHAR TAAL

MAATRA – 17, VIBHAGA – 8, TAALI – 5, KHAALI – 3

THAH

1	2	3	4	5
DHA	TAT	DHA	TIRKIT	DHIN
X		0		2
6	7	8	9	10
NA	TIRKIT	TU	NA	KA
	0		3	
11	12	13	14	15
TA	DHI	DHI	NA	DHI
	4		5	
16	17			
DHI	NA			
0				

DUGUN

1	2	3
DHATAT	DHATIRKIT	DHINA
X		0
4	5	6
TIRKITTU	NAKA	TADHI
	2	
7	8	9
DHINA	DHIDHI	NADHA
0		3
10	11	12
TATDHA	TIRKITDHI	NATIRKIT
		4
13	14	15
TUNA	KATA	DHIDHI
	4	
16	17	
NADHI	DHINA	
0		

TUGUN

1	2	3
DHATATDHA	TIRKITDHINA	TIRKITTUNA
X		0
4	5	6
KATADHI	DHINADHI	DHINADHI
	2	
7	8	9
TATDHATIRKIT	DHINATIRKIT	TUNAKA
0		3
10	11	12
TADHIDHI	NADHIDHI	NADHATAT
		4
13	14	15
DHATIRKITDHI	NATIRKITTU	NAKATA
	5	
16	17	
DHIDHINA	DHIDHINA	
0		

CHOWGUN

1	2
DHATATDHATIRKIT	DHINATIRKITTU
X	
3	4
NAKATADHI	DHINADHIDHI
0	
5	6
NADHATATDHA	TIRKITDHINATIRKIT
2	
7	8
TUNAKATA	DHIDHINADHI
0	
9	10
DHINADHATAT	DHATIRKITDHINA
3	

11
TIRKITTUNAKA

12
TADHIDHINA
4

13
DHIDHINADHA

14
TATDHATIRKITDHI
5

15
NATIRKITTUNA

16
KATADHIDHI
0

17
NADHIDHINA

VISHNU TAAL

MAATRA – 17, VIBHAGA – 8, TAALI – 6, KHAALI – 2

THAH

1	2	3	4	5
DHIN	TIRKIT	DHI	NA	TU
X		0		2
6	7	8	9	10
NA	KA	TA	TIRKIT	DHI
	0		3	
11	12	13	14	15
NA	DHAGE	NADHA	TAK	DHA
4		5		6
16	17			
NADHA	TAK			

DUGUN

1	2	3
DHINTIRKIT	DHINA	TUNA
X		0
4	5	6
KATA	TIRKITDHI	NADHAGE
	2	
7	8	9
NADHATRAK	DHAGENADHA	TAKDHIN
0		3
10	11	12
TIRKITDHI	NATU	NAKA
	4	
13	14	15
TATIRKIT	DHINA	DHAGENADHA
5		6
16	17	
TRAKDHAGE	NADHATAKA	

TUGUN

1	2	3
DHINTIRKITDHI	NATUNA	KATATIRKIT
X		0
4	5	6
DHINADHAGE	NADHATAKDHA	NADHATAKDHIN
	2	
7	8	9
TIRKITDHINA	TUNAKA	TATIRKITDHI
0		3
10	11	12
NADHAGENADHA	TAKDHANADHA	TAKDHINTIRKIT
	4	
13	14	15
DHINATU	NAKATA	TIRKITDHINA
5		
16	17	
DHAGENADHATAK	DHANADHATAK	

CHOWGUN

1	2
DHINTIRKITDHINA	TUNAKATA
X	
3	4
TIRKITDHINADHAGE	NADHATAKDHAGENADHA
0	
5	6
TIAKDHINTIRKITDHI	NATUNAKA
2	
7	8
TATIRKITDHINA	DHAGENADHATAKDHA
0	

9	10
NADHATRAKDHINTIRKIT	DHINATUNA
3	
11	12
KATATIRKITDHI	NADHAGEDHATAK
4	
13	14
DHANADHATAKDHIN	TIRKITDHINATU
5	
15	16
NAKATATIRKIT	DHINADHAGENADHA
6	
17	
TAKDHAGENADHATRAK	

MATT TAAL

MAATRA – 18, VIBHAGA – 9, TAALI – 6, KHAALI – 3

THAH

1	2	3	4	5
DHA	DHA	DIN	TA	KAT
X		0		2
6	7	8	9	10
DHAGE	KAT	DHAGE	DHIN	TA
	3		0	
11	12	13	14	15
KA	TE	TE	DHA	TIT
4		5		6
16	17	18		
KAT	GADI	GAN		
	0			

DUGUN

1	2	3
DHADHA	DINTA	KATDHAGE
X		0
4	5	6
KATDHAGE	DHINTA	KATE
	2	
7	8	9
TEDHA	TITKAT	GADIGAN
3		0
10	11	12
DHADHA	DHINTA	KATDHAGE
	4	
13	14	15
KATDHAGE	DHINTA	KATE
5		6
16	17	18
TEDHA	TITKAT	GADIGAN
	0	

TUGUN

1	2	3
DHADHADIN	TAKATDHAGE	KATDHAGEDHIN
X		0
4	5	6
TAKATE	TEDHATIT	KATGADIGAN
	2	
7	8	9
DHADHADIN	TAKATADHAGE	KATDHAGEDHIN
3		0
10	11	12
TAKATE	TEDHATIT	KATGADHIGAN
	4	
13	14	15
DHADHADIN	TAKATADHAGE	KATADHAGEDHIN
5		6
16	17	18
TAKATE	TEDHATIT	KATGADIGAN
	0	

CHOWGUN

1	2
DHADHADINTA	KATDHAGEKATADHAGE
X	
3	4
DHINTAKATE	TEDHATITKAT
0	
5	6
GADIGANDHADHA	DINTAKATDHAGE
2	
7	8
KATDHAGEDHINTA	KATETEDHA
3	

9	10
TITKATGADIGAN	DHADHADINTA
0	
11	12
KATDHAGEKATDHAGE	DHINTAKATE
4	
13	14
TEDHATITKAT	GADIGANDHADHA
5	
15	16
DHINTAKATADHAGE	KATADHAGEDINTA
6	
17	18
KATETEDHA	TITKATGADIGAN
0	

ARJUNA TAAL

MAATRA – 20, VIBHAGA – 10, TAALI – 7, KHAALI – 3

THAH

1	2	3	4	5
DHA	S	GHE	NA	NA
X		0		2
6	7	8	9	10
KA	GHE	S	GHE	NA
	3		0	
11	12	13	14	15
NA	KA	GHE	S	DHA
4		5		6
16	17	18	19	20
S	GHE	NA	NA	KA
	0		7	

DUGUN

1	2	3	4	5
DHA S	GHENA	NAKA	GHE S	GHENA
X		0		2
6	7	8	9	10
NAKA	GHE S	DHA S	GHENA	NAKA
	3		0	
11	12	13	14	15
DHA S	GHENA	NAKA	GHE S	GHENA
4		5		6
16	17	18	19	20
NAKA	GHE S	DHA S	GHENA	NAKA
	0		7	

TUGUN

1	2	3	4
DHA S GHE	NANAKA	GHE S GHE	NANAKA
X		0	
5	6	7	8
GHE S DHA	S GHENA	NAKADHA	S GHENA
2		3	

9	10	11	12
NAKAGHE	S GHENA	NAKEIGHE	S DHA S
0		4	
13	14	15	16
GHENANA	KADHA S	GHENANA	KAGHE S
5		6	
17	18	19	20
GHENANA	KAGHE S	DHA S GHE	NANAKA
0		7	

CHOWGUN

1	2	3
DHA S GHENA	NAKAGHE S	GHENANAKA
X		0
4	5	6
GHE S DHA S	GHENANAKA	DHA S GHENA
	2	
7	8	9
NAKAGHE S	GHENANAKA	GHE S DHA S
3		0
10	11	12
GHENANAKA	DHA S GHENA	NAKEGHE S
	4	
13	14	15
GHENANAKA	GHE S DHA S	GHENANAKA
5		6
16	17	18
DHA S GHENA	NAKAGHE S	GHENANAKA
	0	
19	20	
GHE S DHA S	GHENANAKA	
7		

GANESHA TAAL

MAATRA –21, VIBHAGA – 10, TAALI – 10

THAH

1	2	3	4	5
DHA	S	KI	TA	TA
X		0		2
6	7	8	9	10
TAA	S	KI	TA	TA
3				4
11	12	13	14	15
KA	DH	DHIN	GA	NA
5	6			
16	17	18	19	20
DHIN	DHA	TA	KA	DHA
7	8	9	10	
21				
TA				

DUGUN

1	2	3	4	5
DHA S	KITA	TATAA	S KI	TATA
X				2
6	7	8	9	10
KADA	DHINGA	NADHIN	DHATA	KADHA
3				4
11	12	13	14	15
TADHA	S KI	TATA	TA S	KIT
5	6			
16	17	18	19	20
TAK	DHADHI	GAN	DHINDHA	TAKA
7	8		9	
21				
DHATA				
10				

TUGUN	1	2	3	4
	DHA S KI	TATATAA	S KITA	TAKADH
	X			
	5	6	7	8
	DHINGAN	DHINDHATA	KADHATA	DHA S KI
	2	3		
	9	10	11	12
	TATATA	S KIT	TAKATDH	DHIGAN
		4	5	6
	13	14	15	16
	DHINDHAT	KADHATA	DHA S KI	TATATAA
				7
	17	18	19	20
	S KITA	TAKADH	DHINGANA	DHINDHATA
	8	9	10	
	21			
	KADHATA			

CHOWGUN	1	2	3
	DHA S KIT	TATAASKE	TATAKADH
	X		
	4	5	6
	DHINGANADHIN	DHATAKADHA	TADHASKI
		2	3
	7	8	9
	TATATAAS	KITATHKA	DHDHINGANA
	10	11	12
	DHINDHATAKA	DHATADHA S	KITATATAA
	4	5	6
	13	14	15
	SKITATA	KADHDHINGA	NADHINDHATA
	16	17	18
	KADHATADHA	SKITATA	TAASKITA
	7	8	9
	19	20	21
	TAKADHDHIN	GANDINDHA	TKADHATA
	10		

2. DANCE NOTATIONS IN JHAPTAAL

THATH

1.

S THEI	S TA	S THEI	SS	S THEI
X		2		
S TA	S THEI	SS S THEI	S TA	
0				
THEI				
X				

I1.

12345	12 S	12345	12 S	12345
X		2		
12 S	12345	12345	THEITHEI	TAT
0		3		
TA				
X				

AMAD

TA	THEI	TAT	SS	AA
X		2		
THEI	TAT	SS	THEI	EIS
0		3		
THEI	EIS	TAT	TAT	TA
X		2		
TAT	TAT	TA	TAT	TAT
0		3		
TA				
X				

NATVARI

TAT	TAT	TIGDA	DIGDIG	TIGDA
X		2		
DIGDIG	TAT	TAT	THEI	YATHA
0		3		
EEYA	KARA	TIGDA	DIGDIG	THEI
X		2		
TIGDA	DIGDIG	THEI	TIGDA	DIGDIG
0		3		
THEI				
X				

PARAN AMAD

TA	DHATA	KATHUN	GA S	DHAGE
X		2		
DHINGA	TA	DHADHIN	TA	DHITTA
0		3		
KIT S DHA	TAKKA	THUNGA	TAKITATA	KA S TA S
X		2		
DHA	TITKAT	GADIGAN	DHA	TAKITATA
0		3		
KA S TA	DHA S	TITKAT	GADIGAN	DHA S
X		2		
TAKITATA	KA S TA	DHA S	TITKAT	GADIGAN
0		3		
DHA				
X				

TUKDA

TATTAT	THEI	TIGADADIGDIG	THEI	TATAT
X		2		
THEI	TIGDADIGDIG	THEI	TA S THEI	TA S THEI
0		3		
THEITATHEI S	TATHEI	THEITHEI	TATTAT	DHA S
X		2		
NADHA	S NA	DHA	NADHA	S NA
0		3		
DHA				
X				

PARAN

DHAGETIT	DHAGETIT	TAGETIT
X		2
TAGETIT	KITDHATIT	DHAGETIT
		0
TITKATGADIGAN	DHA S TITKAT	GADIGANDHA
	3	
S TITKATGADIGAN	DHA	
	X	

CHAKKARDAAR TUKDA

TIDA S TI	DA S THEI	THEIKARAN
X		2
DHA S KAT	DHA S KARAN	DHAKAT
		0
DHAKARAN	DHA S KAT	DHA
	3	

SS	SS X	TIDA S TI
DHA S THEI 2	THEIKARAN	DHA S KAT
DHAKARAN 0	DHA S KAT	DHA S KARAN 3
DHASKAT	DHASS X	SS
TIDA S TI 2	DHA S THEI	THEIKARAN
DHA S KAT 0	DHAKARN	DHA S KAT 3
DHAKARAN	DHA SKAT	DHA X

KAVITH

AASPA X	EASMAE	GOPIYAN 2
NA S CH	NRITYAKA	RATDHAN 0
SHYA S M	S DHAN 3	SHYA S M
S DHANSHYAS M	MA X	

CHAKKARDAAR PARAN

GADIGAN	NAGETIT	TAGETIRKIT	TAKDHIKIT
0		3	
DHA S NATA	DHATA	DHAKITDHA	TITDHA
	X		2
S NADHA S	DHAKITDHA S	TTDHA	S NADHA S
		0	
DHAKITDHA	TITDHA S	S NADHA S	DHADIGAN
3			X
NAGETIT	TAGETIRKIT	TAKDHIKIT	DHA S NATA
	2		
DHATA	DHAKITDHA	TITDHA	S NADHA S
0		3	
DHAKITDHA S	TITDHA	S NADHA S	DHAKITDHA
	X		2
TITDHA S	S NADHA S	DHAGADIGAN	NAGETIT
		0	
TAGETIRKIT	TAKDHIKIT	DHA S NATA	DHATA
3			X
DHAKITDHA	TITDHA	S NADHA S	DHAKITDHA S
	2		
TITDHA	S NADHA S	DHAKITDHA	TITDHA S
0		3	
S NADHA S	DHA		
	X		

TIHAI

I.

TAKITATA	TAKITATA	GINTAKIT	GINTAKIT
0		2	
DHA	TAKITATA	TAKITATA	GINTAKIT
	X		2
GINTAKIT	DHA	TAKITATA	TAKITATA
		0	
GINTAKIT	GINTAKIT	DHA	
3			

II.

TIGDADIGDIG X	TIGDADIGDIG	123 2
TIGDADIGDIG	TIGDADIGDIG	12345 0
TIGDADIGDIG	TIGDADIGDIG 3	1234567
TA S KIT	TIGDADIGDIG X	TIGDADIGDIG
123 2	TIGDADIGDIG	TIGDADIGDIG
12345 0	TIGDADIGDIG	TIGDADIGDIG 3
1234567	TA S KIT	TIGDADIGDIG X
TIGDADIGDIG	123 2	TIGDADIGDIG
TIGDADIGDIG	12345 0	TIGDADIGDIG
TIGDADIGDIG 3	1234567	TA S KIT

3. DANCE NOTATIONS IN EKTAAL

THATH

1	2	3	4	5
X		0		2
6	7	8	9	10
	0	THEITA	THEI	TA
			3	
11	12			
THEITHEI	TAT	TA		
4		X		

AMAD

TATHEI	TATTHEI	AATHEI	TATTHEI
X		0	
THEI S	THEI S	THEI SSS	TATTAT
2		0	
TA	TATTAT	TA	TATTAT
3		4	
TA			
X			

PARAN AMAD

DHATA	KATHUN	GA S	DHAGE
X		0	
DHING	TA	DHADHIN	TA
2		0	
DHITA	KITDHA	TAKKA	THUNGA
3		4	
TAKITTA	KA S DHA	TITKAT	GADIGAN
X		0	
DHA S TA S	DHA S TIT	KATGADI	GANDHA
2		0	
TADHA	TITKAT	GADIGAN	DHA S TA
3		4	
DHA			
X			

NATVARI TUKDA

TAT X	TAT	TIGDHA 0	DIGDIG
TIGDHA 2	DIGDIG	TAT 0	TAT
THEI 3	YATHE	IYA 4	KRAN
TATTAT X	TIGDADIGDIG	TIGDADIGDIG 0	TATTAT
THEI 2	TIGDADIGDIG	TIGDADIGDIG 0	TATTAT
THEI 3	TIGADADIGDIG	TIGDADIGDIG 4	TATTAT
THEI X			

TUKDA

TATHEI X	TATTHEI	AATHEI 0	TATTHEI
THEIATHE 2	EIATHEI	THEITHEI 0	TATTAT
TA S TAT 3	TATTA	S TATTAT 4	TA

KAVITH

UJAKAT X	JHIJHIKAT	JHUKATU 0	CHALHAL
CHANDRACH 2	PALCHAP	LASSAM 0	AACHAPAL
LACHKIL 3	CHAKIKATEE	MATKIM 4	DAKIMUKH
MAND S HA X	SATMAN	MOHAN 0	MANMA

DHO S 2	SS MAN	MOHANM 0	A NMA **A**
DHO S 3	SS MAN	MO S HAN 4	MANMA
DHO X			

CHAKKARDAAR TUKDA

TATHEI X	TATTHEI	AATHEI 0	TATTHEI
THEITATHA 2	EITHEI	THEITHEI 0	TATTAT
TA S TAT 3	THEITHEI	TATTAT 4	TA S TAT
THEITHEI X	TATTAT	TA SS 0	SS
SS 2	TATTHEI	TATTHEI 0	AATHEI
TATHEI 3	THEITHA	EITHEI 4	THEITHEI
TATTAT X	TA S TAT	THEITHEI 0	TATTAT
TA S TAT 2	THEITHEI	TATTAT 0	TA S
SS 3	SS	TATHEI 4	TATTHEI
AATHEI X	TATTHEI	THEITA 0	EITHEI
THEITHEI 2	TATTAT	TA S TAT 0	THEITHEI
TATTAT 3	TA S TAT	THEITHEI 4	TATTAT
TA S X			

PARAN

DHETDHET	TRAKDHET	DHETDHET	TRAKDHET
X		0	
TAGANNA	DHETTA	TAGANNA	DHETTA
2		0	
DHETDHET	TAGHEGHE	TITKAT	GADIGAN
3		4	
DHATA	DHATA	DHAGHEGHE	TITKAT
X		0	
GADIGAN	DHATA	DHATA	DHAGHEGHE
2		0	
TITKAT	GADIGAN	DHATA	DHATA
3		4	
DHA			
X			

CHAKKARDAAR PARAN

GADIGAN	NAGETIT	TAGETIR	KITTAK
X		0	
DHAKITDHA	S NATA S	DHA	TADHA
2		0	
S TA	DHAKIRDHA	TITDHA S	NADHA S NA
3		4	
DHA S KIRDHA	TITDHA S	NADHA S	DHA S KIRDHA
X		0	
TITDHA	NADHA S NA	DHA	SS
2		0	
SS	GADIGAN	NAGETIT	TAGETIR
3		4	
KITTAT	DHADHITDHA	S NATA	DHA
X		0	
TADHA	S TA	- DHA S KIRDHA	TITDHA S
2		0	

NADHA S NA	DHA S KIRDHA	TITDHA S	NADHA S NA
3		4	
DHA S KIRDHA	TITDHA	NADHA S NA	DHA
X		0	
SS	SS	GADIGAN	NAGETIT
2		0	
TAGETIR	KITTAK	DHAKITDHA	S NATA S
3		4	
DHA S	TADHA	STA	DHA S KIRDHA
X		0	
TITDHA S	NADHA S NA	DHA S KIRDHA	TITDHA
2		0	
NADHA S NA	DHA S KIRDHA	TITDHA S	NADHA S NA
3		4	
DHA			
X			

TIHAI

I.

TIGDADIGDIG	TIGDADIGDIG	THEITA	THEI S
X		0	
TIGDADIGDIG	TIGDADIGDIG	THEITA	THEI S
2		0	
TIGDADIGDIG	TIGDADIGDIG	THEITA	THEI
3		4	

II.

TIGDADIGDIG	TIGDADIGDIG	12345	S THEI S
X		0	
TIGDADIGDIG	TIGDADIGDIG	12345	S THEI S
2		0	
TIGDADIGDIG	TIGDADIGDIG	12345	S THEI S
3		4	

4. DANCE NOTATIONS IN DHAMAAR

THATH

I.	1	2	3	4	5
	X				
	6	7	8		
		THEITA	THEI	SS	TA
	2		0		
	11	12	13	14	
	SS	THEI S	THEI SS	T S T	TA
					X
II.	1	2	3	4	5
	X				
	6	7	8	9	10
			THEITA	THEI	TATHEI
	2		0		
	11	12	13	14	
	S TA	THEITHEI	S TA	TA	TA
	3				X

AMAD

TA	THEI	TAT	SS	AA
X				
THEI	TAT	SS	THEI	SS
2		0		
THEI	SSS	TAT	TAT	TA
3				X

NATVARI TUKDA

TATTAT	TIGDADIGDIG	TIGDADIGDIG	TATTAT
X			
THEIYATHE	IYAKRAN	TATTAT	TIGDADIGDIG
	2		0
THEI 1	2 3	TIGDADIGDIG	THEI 1
		3	
2 3	TIGDADIGDIG	TA	
		X	

II.

THEITHEI	TATTAT	TA S	SS
X			
THEITTE	ETHEI	THEITHEI	TATTAT
	2		0
TA S	SS	THEITTE	EITHEI
		3	
THEITHEI	TATTAT	TA	
		X	

PARAN AMAD

DHATA	KATHUN	GA S	DHAGE
X			
DHING	TA S	DHADHIN	TA S
	2		0
DHITA	KITDHA	TAKKA	THUNGA
		3	
TAKITTA	KA	TITKATGADIGAN	TATHEI
		X	
TATTHEI	AATHEI	TATTHEI	THEITATHE
		2	
EITHEI	THEITHEI	TATTAT	TA S
0			3
S TAT	TATTA SS	TATTAT	TA
			X

TUKDA

TATTAT X	THEI	TIGDADIGDIG	THEI
TATTAT	THEI 2	TIGDADIGDIG	THEI 0
TATHEI	TATHEI	AATHEI 3	TATTHEI
THEITA	EITHEI		

CHAKKARDAAR TUKDA

TATTAT X	THEI	TIGDADIGDIG	THEI
TATTAT	THEI 2	TIGDADIGDIG	THEI 0
TATHEI	TATHEI	AATHEI 3	TATTHEI
THEITT	EITHEI	THEITHEI X	TATTAT
TA S	SS	THEITT	EITHEI 2
THEITHEI	TATTAT 0	TA S	SS
THEITT 3	EITHEI	THEITHEI	TATTAT
TATTATTAT X	THEI	TIGDADIGDIG	THEI
TATTAT	THEI 2	TIGDADIGDIG	THEI 0
TATHEI	TATTHEI	AATHEI 3	TATTHEI
THEITTA	EITHEI	THEITHEI X	TATTAT

TA S	SS	THEIATT	EITHEI
			2
THEITHEI	TATTAT	TA S	SS
	0		
THEITATA	EIATHEI	THEITHEI	TATTAT
3			
TATTATTAT	THEI	TIGDADIGDIG	THEI
X			
TATTAT	THEI	TIGDADIGDIG	THEI
	2		0
TATHEI	TATHEI	AATHEI	TATHEI
		3	
THEITTA	EIATHEI	THEITHEI	TATTAT
		X	
TA S	SS	THEIATT	EIATHEI
			2
THEITHEI	TATTAT	TA S	SS
	0		
THEIATT	EIATHEI	THEITHEI	TATTAT
3			
TA			
X			

PARAN

DHETDHET	TAGANNA	DHETTA
X		
TAGANNA	DHETTA	KARA S NA
		2
KARA S NA	DHAKARA S NA	KARA S NADHA S
	0	
TITKATGADIGAN	DHA S	TITKATGADIGAN
	3	
DHA S	TITKATGADIGAN	DHA
		X

KAVITH

VRINDA S	VANKE S	SAGANKUN	SAJME S
X			
KADMAT	RUTATLAY S	SHYAMK	ANAYA S
	2		0
BAJAYE S	BAN S SI S	BAJAYE S	BAN S SI S
		3	
BAJAYE S	BAN S SI S	RE SSS	BAJAYE S
		X	
BAN S SI S	BAJAYE S	BAN S SI S	BAJAYE S
			0
BAN S SI S	RE SSS	BAJAYE S	BAN S SI S
	2		
BAJAYE S	BAN S SI S	RE	
3		X	

CHAKKARDAAR PARAN

DHETHDET	TAGANNA	DHETTA
TAGANNA	DHETTA	KARA S NA
		2
KARA S NA	DHA S KARA S NA	KARA S NADHA S
	0	
TITKATGADIGAN	DHA S	TITKATGADIGAN
	3	
DHA S	TITKATGADIGAN	DHADHETHDET
		X
TAGANNA	DHETTA	TAGANNA
DHETTA	KARA S NA	KARA S NA
	2	

DHA S KARA S NA 0	KARA S NADHA S	TITKATGADIGAN
DHA S 3	TITKATGADIGAN	DHA S
TITKATGADIGAN	DHADHETDHET X	TAGANNA
DHETTA	TAGANNA	DHETTA
KARA S NA 2	KARA S NA	DHA S KARAN S NA 0
KARA S NADHA A	TITKATGADIGAN	DHA S 3
TITKATGADIGAN	DHA S	TITKATGADIGAN
DHA X		

TIHAI

TIGDADIGDIG X	THEIAT	THEIAT
THEIAT	THEI	TIGDADIGDIG 2
THEIAT	THEIAT 0	THEIAT
THEI	TIGDADIGDIG 3	THEIAT
THEIAT	THEIAT	THEI X

5. DANCE NOTATIONS IN PANCHAMSAWARI

THATH

I.	1	2	3	4	5
	X			2	
	6	7	8	9	10
			0		
	11	12	13	14	15
		THEITA	THEI	TAT	TAT
	3				
	TA				
	X				

II.	1	2	3	4	5
				S THEI	TATE
	X			2	
	6	7	8	9	10
	EIAT	THEI	TA	THEI	TATE
	2		0		
	11	12	13	14	15
	EIAT	THEI	TATHEI	STA	STA
	3				
	16				
	TA				
	X				

AMAD

TA	THEI	TAT	SS	AA
X			2	
THEI	TAT	THEI	SS	THEI
		0		
SS	THEI	SS	TAT	TAT
	3			
TA				
X				

TUKDA

TRAMTAK	TRAMTAK	TIGDADIGDIG	TIGDADIGDIG
X			2
THEITHEI	THEIAT	THEIAT	THEIAT
			0
THEI	TATHEI	TATHEI	TATHEI
			3
TAT	THEITAT	THEITAT	THEI
			X

CHAKKARDAAR TUKDA

DHEDHETIT	DHEDHETIT	KATKAT	KAT S
X			2
THEITHEI	THEI S	TIGDADIGDIG	TIGDADIGDIG
			0
THEIATH	EIATHEI	THEITRAM	THEITRAM
			3
DHADHAKIT	DHADHAKIT	DHITDHA	S DHITDHA
			X
THEIATH	EITHEI	TIGDADIGDIG	THEITRAM
		2	
THEI S	THEIATHE	EITHEI	TIGDADIGDIG
		0	
HEITRAM	THEI SS	THEIATHE	EITHEI
		3	
ADIGDIG	THEITRAM	THEI	
		X	

KAVITH

I.

CHANDRACH X	PALKAR	AR S TI
SHIVKE S 2	JHIJHIKAT	HULHUL
GAN S TA	CHALKAT 0	NA S CAT
SHANKAR	THATHAAN	KITTATTHUNTHUN 3
DHA S KITTAK	THUNTHUNDHA S	KITTATTHUNTHUN
DHA X		

PARAN AMAD

DHATA X	KATHUN	GA S
DHAGE 2	DHING	TA S
DHADHIN	TA S 0	DHIT
TA	KIT	DHA 3
TAT	KA	THUN
GA X	TAKITA	KA
TITKAT 2	GADIGAN	DHA S TA
DHA	1 2 TIT 0	KATGADI
GANDHA S	TADHA	1 2 3
TITKAT	GADIGAN	DHA S TA
DHA X		

PARAN

DHAGETIT X	DHAGETIT	KIRDHATIT
DHAGETIT 2	GADIGAN	NAGETIT
TAGANNA	DHETTA 0	TAGANNA
DHETTA	TITKATGADIGAN	DHA SS 3
TITKATGADIGAN	DHA SS	TITKATGADIGAN
DHA X		

TIHAI

TIGDA X	DIGDIG	TIGDA
DIGDIG 2	THEI S	TIGDA
DIGDIG	THEI S 0	TIGDA
DIGDIG	THEI S	TIGDA 3
DIGDIG	TIGDA	DIGDIG
THEI X		

II.

THIRAKTHI X	RAKPAG	DHARATJA
S TASAKHI 2	GHUNGHAT	SIRAPA S
RASARAKJA	SATMRUG 0	NAYANI

CHANCHAL	MANLUBHA	S TARAS 3
DHA SS	RADHA	S RA
DHA X		

CHAKKARDAAR PARAN

DHETDHET X	TRAKDHET	S TRAK
DHET S 2	DHETDHET	TRAKDHET
S TRAK	DHET S 0	TAGANNA
DHETA	DHETDHET	TA 3
TITKAT	GADIGAN	DHATIT
KATGADI X	GANDHA	TITKAT
GADIGAN 2	DHA	DHET
DHETTRAK	DHET S 0	TRAKDHET
S DHET	DHETTRAK	DHET S 3
TRAKDHET	S TAG	NNADHE
TA S DHET X	DHETTA	S TIT
KATGADI 2	GANDHA	TITKAT
GADIGAN	DHATIT 0	KATGADI

GANDHA	----	DHETDHET 3
TRAKDHET	STRAK	DHET S
DHETDHET X	TRAKDHET	S TRAK
DHET S 2	TAGANNA	DHE S TA S
DHETDHET	TA S 0	TITKAT
GADIGAN	DHA S TET	KATGADI
GANDHA S	TITKAT	GADIGAN
DHA		

THEI S	YA S	THEIYA	KRAN
0			
TATTAT	TIGDADIGDIG	TIGDADIGDIG	TATTAT
3			
TA			
X			

TUKDA

DIGDIG	DIGDIG	THEI	SS	TATHE
X				2
ITA	THEI	S THE	EI S	TAT
			0	
THO S	SS	DIGDIG	DIGDIG	THEI
			3	
SS	TATHE	ITA	THEI	S THE
	X			
I S	TAT	THO	SS	TIGDA S
2				0
DA S TIG	DA S DA S	DIGDIG	TIGDA S	DA S TIG
			3	
DA S DA S	THO S	TIGDA	DA S TIG	DA S DAD
		X		
DIGDIG	TIGDA S	DA S TIG	DA S DA S	DIGDIG
	2			
TATHE	ITA	AATHE	ITA	TATHE
0				3
ITA	SS TIG	DA S TA S	TO	
			X	

KAVITH

JHATA	S JHU	SAT	MADHE	GANG S
X				2
GAK	LAK	KAT	SHEAD	SHACHA
			0	

S DRA	LIL	LA S 3	TAM	LAK
KAT	MU S X	S MA	S LA	GALAE
SHA S 2	S HD	RATHE	DHAR	PA S 0
RAB	ATI S	PATI	SHIV 3	HAR
HAR	HAR	PA S X	RAB	ATI S
PATI	SHIV 2	HAR	HAR	HAR
PA S 0	RAB	AT S	PATI	SHIV 3
HAR	HAR	HAR		

CHAKKARDAAR TUKDA

TA S THEI X	TATTHEI	AATHEI	TATTHEI
THEIATTH 2	EIATHEI	THEITHEI	TATTAT
TA S 0	TATTAT	TA S	TATTAT
TA 3	SS	THEIATH	EITHEI
THEITHEI X	TATTAT	TA S	TATTAT
TA S 2	TATTAT	TA	SS
THEIATH 0	EIATHEI	THEITHEI	TATAT

TA S	TATTAT	TA S	TATTAT
3			
TA			
X			

PIRMALU TUKDA

TA SSS	THUNGA	TAKKA	THU S NGA S
X			
TIGDHE S	S TA S	THU S GA	TAKKA S
2			
DIGDIG	DIGDIG	DIGDIG	THEI SS
0			
TATTAT	THEITAT	TATTHEI	TATTAT
3			
THEI			
X			

CHAKKARDAAR PARAN

GADIGAN	NAGETIT	TAGETIR	KITTAK
X			
DAKITDHA	NATADHA	TADHA	KITDHATIT
2			
DHANDHAN	DHA S	KITDHATIT	DHANDHAN
0			
DHA S	KITDHATIT	DHANDHAN	DHA
3			
GADIGAN	NAGETIT	TAGETIR	KITTAK
X			
DAKITDHA	NATADHA	TADHA	KITDHATIT
2			
DHANDHAN	DHA S	KITDHATIT	DHANDHAN
0			
DHA S	KITDHATIT	DHANDHAN	DHA
3			

GADIGAN	NAGETIT	TAGETIR	KITTAK
X			
DAKITDHA	NATADHA	TADHA	KITDHATIT
2			
DHANDHAN	DHA S	KITDHATIT	DHANDHAN
0			
DHA S	KITDHATIT	DHANDHAN	DHA
3			

TIHAI

9	10	11
TAKITTA S	TAKITTA S	TAKITTAKIT
0		
12	13	14
THEI SS	TAKITTA S	TAKITTA S
15	16	
TAKITTAKIT	THEI	

II.

TIGADADIGDIG	TIGADADIGDIG	THEITA
X		
THEITA	THEI	S
	2	
TIGADADIGDIG	TIGADADIGDIG	THEITA
		0
THEITA	THEI	S
TIGADADIGDIG	TIGDA S DIGDIG	THEITA
3		
THEITA	THEI	
	X	

●●●